D1389741

BATH SPA UNIVERSITY COLLEGE
SION HILL LIBRARY

Please return or renew not later than
the latest date stamped below

JAPANESE MASTERS
OF THE COLOUR PRINT

PHAIDON

UTAGAWA TOYOKUNI: *Iwai Hanshirō in a feminine rôle.* About 1794

JAPANESE MASTERS
OF THE COLOUR PRINT

A Great Heritage of Oriental Art

J. HILLIER

PHAIDON

FOREWORD

FOR us in this country, the opportunities of an acquaintance with Japanese art are few. Although there are galleries in practically every large town where the works of European schools can be studied, there is no permanent exhibition of Japanese painting anywhere, and in any case, though the British Museum has a fairly representative collection that can be studied on application, most of the finest examples of Japanese painting remain in Japan. It is not surprising, therefore, that when, on rare occasions, a Japanese picture, or a reproduction of one, is seen, it impinges itself on most people as something unintelligible, remote from our own art, portraying in a strange stylistic manner a world where custom and dress, legend and history, and even the physiognomy of the inhabitants, are unfamiliar.

Yet to those who study the art of Japan, this foreignness of style and subject soon ceases to be an obstacle to appreciation. Indeed, though the subject matter may remain uninterpreted, the style is found to be an exposition of the highest ideals of the art of painting, vying in its own idiom with the greatest painting of Italy and France, and anticipating by hundreds of years, and enjoying by right, the freedom from the 'tyranny of nature' so hardly won by modern European artists since Cézanne.

Though the actual paintings of Japan are so far out of reach, the colour-prints of the country are fortunately more accessible; the British Museum and the Victoria and Albert Museum, the Museum of Fine Arts in Boston, the Art Institute of Chicago, the Wadsworth Atheneum in Hartford and the New York Public Library contain many fine prints, and many still pass through the hands of art-dealers and auctioneers. It is true that these prints are the product of a relatively humble school that came late into being in the Seventeenth Century, and whose finest works in no sense realize the highest aims of Japanese art: but for us, they provide a gateway, an easy initiation into an art that to many may seem forbidding, not only from its foreignness, but from the austerity of its lofty conceptions. There are those who may eventually scale those ultimate peaks, but others will rest content with the pleasures of the lower slopes.

But even these prints, woodcuts printed in colours and bought by the masses, at once delightful to our eyes and needing little adjustment of our normal focus for them to yield real aesthetic pleasure, even these have for long been known only to the minority. Literature on the subject has generally been intended more for collectors than for the general art-lover and has assumed as a rule far more advanced a knowledge of Oriental art than the average reader, for the reasons

5

given, has been able to acquire. Moreover, except in the most expensive editions, books on the colour-print have been illustrated very inadequately.

In this introductory book, the aim has been to present the colour-print as an art, rooted in the principles of Japanese painting but needing for its appreciation no deep knowledge of those principles, examples being selected for reproduction not so much for their rarity as their power to bring home the unique qualities of Japanese art and especially of the colour-print art. Similarly, the text deals with the subject in general terms, sketching the character of the people for whom the prints were brought into being; the development of the artists' style; and some of the causes for its distinctiveness from all we are used to in European art.

Short biographies of the major artists associated with the colour-print are given in an Appendix. Signatures of these artists and their principal pupils are given in another to meet a generally felt need, especially among new collectors, one of whose first desires is to identify the artists, to associate a personality, however slightly known, with the work of art.

J.H.

INTRODUCTION

THE PICTORIAL ART OF JAPAN

THE colour-print was in the main, though not exclusively, the product of a certain school of painters that arose in the Seventeenth Century, whose methods were considered sufficiently different from those of the established schools to earn a name of its own, the *Ukiyo-ye*, or 'Pictures of the Fleeting World' School. But although that title, with its hint of opprobrium, suggesting as it does a concern with the petty things of everyday life in contrast to the 'eternal verities' that engaged followers of older schools, distinguishes a quite clearly separate style of Japanese painting, that style is still essentially Japanese, and an explanation of certain of the characteristics of the colour-print best begins in a general consideration of the art of painting as practised in Japan. A comparison, at the same time, with Western art, gives an opportunity to deal with some of the objections to Japanese art which are almost inevitably raised by those steeped in the Western traditions who approach it for the first time. Perhaps 'comparison' is hardly an accurate term where such incompatibles are concerned, for though identical in that both are pictorial means of expression, the gulf between them is deeper than the Pacific.

Japanese painting is more limited in range than European: but more perfect within its proscribed limits. Its limitations were due in part to the restricted media and opportunities open to the Japanese compared with those available to the Western artists, to whom the advent of oil-painting gave possibilities of expression never accepted by the Japanese, or, as some would say, wisely eschewed by them. It is true that modern Japanese artists have used oils, but in doing so they have adopted European methods, and in any consideration of the art of their country one refers to the products of the purely native schools, Kano, Tosa, Kōrin, Shijō— a Japanese, painting in a Western style, loses his national identity as completely as his countryman who forsakes the kimono for the lounge suit.

Oddly enough, the choice of media was imposed on the Japanese as much by geological and climatic factors as by any innate artistic preference or instinct: the flimsy construction of their buildings, dictated by the recurrence of earthquakes and leading to frequent conflagrations, precluded anything like the great wall spaces enjoyed by the early European painters in fresco and tempera, or even the solid frame and robust canvas normal to our oil painters. Instead, they used water-colours on silk and paper, materials which, in the characteristic *makemono* and *kakemono* forms (the first a long horizontal, the other a tall vertical, oblong), could be rolled up and moved to a place of safety, where for the most part of the year they were stored.

This use of water-colour, and later of wood-engraving printed in colours, tended to stand in the way, if there had been any movement in that direction, of any laborious technique which might have led, as the oil-painting technique did in

Europe, to the mimicry of visual appearances. But water-colour *could* have been turned to this copy-work—after all, Birket Foster used identical materials: but from the first, the Japanese genius was for the expressive line, for pattern and design, the representation of natural objects as a means to an end, not an end in itself. Chiaroscuro and linear perspective, used by western artists to give the verisimilitude of solidity in natural objects and their recession in space, were ignored, though not unknown. They did not 'draw from nature' as we are, or were, taught to, but stored images in the mind until the mood was upon them to paint: with them, painting, like poetry, was the 'spontaneous overflow of power-ful feelings' and took its origin from 'emotion recollected in tranquillity'.

Fundamentally, the difference between Japanese and Western art lies not so much in media or technique as in the aim of the artists, the conception of the function of painting. With us, until comparatively modern times, the art of painting was tied to some underlying purpose of decoration, story-telling, por-trayal of people or chronicling of events. Progress was measured by the closer and still closer approximation to the appearances of things, Ruskin typifying that form of art criticism that uses 'truth to nature' as the yardstick to measure a painter's stature. True, since Ruskin and the invention of photography, there has been a growing realization that the art of painting should reside in something more than the simple aim of imitation (contact with the art of the East from the Nineteenth Century onwards almost certainly speeded that realization), but until then, European painting was descriptive or objective, often the dependent of the sister art of architecture, often fulfilling the function that a camera fulfils today. The paintings of El Greco and William Blake, to name two at least who are excep-tions to the rule, have qualities which even now do not find general acceptance among us.

The work of the Japanese painter, unhampered by the external considerations that pressed upon the European, was valued for the 'beauty and significance of touch', the actual brush-strokes, the arabesque of their line, having, for people who appraised chirography as one of the fine arts, an appeal that we learn but slowly to appreciate; and conveyed, to the well-stocked mind, not directly but by hints and allusions, a whole world of meaning lost upon us. There is nothing in their art akin to the portraiture of Reynolds, still less of Rembrandt or Velasquez; no landscapes of the fidelity to topography and atmosphere that Constable, Turner or Monet achieved; little of the allegorical, narrative or didactic painting, the 'sermons in paint' which, on wall and canvas, from Giotto to Brangwyn, have been accepted as one of the functions of the art in the West. Theirs was an art in which line and hue and *notan* were evocative in the way that a word, or a turn of phrase, is evocative in our poetry. Laurence Binyon, referring to the classic Kano school, wrote: 'The one thing necessary for a work of art was that it should bring with it the fertilising seed to come to flower in the beholder's mind: the thought of the artist was to enter like a guest into a room made ready for his welcome'.

8

THE ORIGIN OF THE COLOUR-PRINT

It can readily be imagined that even among the Japanese such an art could only be addressed to those of a culture comparable to that of the artists, and in fact its appreciation was restricted to the aristocratic minority of the nation. The art of the Ukiyo-ye, of the colour-print artists, was, on the other hand, the art of a popular school, and for that reason if for no other, the colour-prints are more readily enjoyed by us than the works of the earlier masters: indeed, though their allegiance is decidedly to the East, they seem to occupy a sort of border state between East and West, with an artistic climate more nearly approaching our own, and whence we can approach by an easy gradient to the more difficult peaks, the rarefied atmosphere, of the ancient classical art.

The advent of such a popular art was bound up with great social changes, and was dependent on the emergence of a class of people that had no previous counterpart. After generations of internecine struggles, the firm rule of the Tokugawa Shogunate, first installed to power at the beginning of the Seventeenth Century, brought stability and prosperity to the troubled country, and the population of the new capital, Yedo, grew rapidly. Education was more widely disseminated than ever before, and a middle class of tradesmen, artisans and merchants emerged, quick-witted, intelligent, pleasure-loving and avid for novelty. It was for this parvenu class that the *Kabuki*, or Popular, Drama, the Marionette Theatre, and an immensely varied and voluminous literature came into being, and it was to illustrate the publications of the day that the first Ukiyo-ye woodcuts were made. Before considering the gradual development of the colour-print from these first beginnings, it is well to go a little deeper into a question of paramount importance in Japanese art—Style.

THE UKIYO-YE STYLE

Consistent with the acceptance of painting as an art in its own right, styles of painting in Japan are differentiated more on the grounds of brushwork than on the type of subject-matter. The Ukiyo-ye style is primarily a style of *painting*, first introduced in the mid-Seventeenth Century by an artist named Matahei, and followed, with developments, by all the major artists of the school. These paintings comprised, in Japanese estimation, the most important part of their *oeuvre*. In the make-up of their style are elements borrowed from both the Tosa and the Kano schools, the vivid opaque colour of the one, the strong forceful bounding lines of the other, but the amalgam is quite distinct from either of the early styles, and moreover, the class of subject depicted, something approaching a Japanese *genre*, had only occasionally appeared before.

But the paintings, executed for the wealthier patrons only, were relatively few in number: the style was first devoted to popular ends by an artist of the name of Moronobu, and it is his prolific illustrations to books, and later separately issued broadsheets, that initiated a style in drawing for the woodcut and a range of

9

Fig. 1. HISHIKAWA MORONOBU: *A page from the picture-book* Musashi Yehon. About 1680. (8 × 6 in.)

subject-matter that affected the whole history of the colour-print.

In a selection of prints such as those reproduced here, one of the most striking features is the oneness of the style that, for all the developments in technique and the following of changing fashions in dress and manners, informs the work of artists of widely separated periods. The exceptions are to be found in the essays in the Kano or Chinese styles that occasionally occur; in the flirting with European methods in such prints as the 'perspective pictures' known as *Uki-ye*; and in some phases of the work of Hokusai, whose eclecticism, his assimilation of the styles of a variety of schools, renders some of his prints barely classifiable as Ukiyo-ye, notwithstanding the colour-print medium.

Without a comparison, not possible here, with the other various styles of Japanese painting, it is rather difficult to bring home the characteristics that single out a Ukiyo-ye drawing from that in any other style: but suffice to say that there is an immediately obvious kinship, notwithstanding the differences already noted, between the drawings of a woman by such diversely gifted artists as Moronobu, Kwaigetsudō, Okumura Masanobu, Harunobu or Kiyonaga, and an equally clear distinction between their drawings and those of a Kano or Tosa master. Although the Ukiyo-ye style was based on both the Kano and the Tosa, its suave flowing lines are never mistakable for the impetuous, splintery strokes of the Kano masters, and the lively near-naturalism of its figure-painting is a world apart from the stiff, ritualistic manner of the Tosa.

This continuity of a style through generation after generation of artists was the result of the method of training. A pupil accepted by one of the masters was like the apprentice to any other craftsman: he followed implicitly the instructions of the master, reproduced his productions as closely as possible. We in the West, at any rate since mediaeval times, have no parallel to the rule and authority exercised by the Japanese painter over his pupil: not only had the main tenets of the school of adoption to be respected, but the particular idiosyncrasies of the sub-school in which the young artist had enrolled had to be followed with complete fidelity. Hence the great similarity—the impossibility of telling apart, quite often—

of the prints, say, of Harunobu and his pupils (one named Shiba Kōkan openly confessed to forging Harunobu's signature, and no two experts have ever agreed as to which are the forgeries) of Shunshō and those of his pupils who produced theatrical prints; of Kiyonaga and all those that fell under his sway, such as Shunchō and Yeishi.

Without knowing the prints, it might be inferred that such a system could only lead to servile copying and stagnation, but, in fact, the reverse was the case. Each great artist, and there was a constant succession of them, beginning as an imitator of his master, developed an individuality in drawing and treatment of subject, that stamps his prints as plainly as the signature or seal upon them: and that he, in his turn, was successfully imitated by his successors, only emphasizes his distinctive achievement as an innovator.

In perhaps no other aspect can this be made clearer than in the drawing of women, to whom, above all, the Ukiyo-ye artists devoted their work. The small, compactly-drawn figures of Moronobu are given imposing build and monumental pose in the massive lines of Kwaigetsudō and Kiyonobu; Okumura Masanobu and Sukenobu infuse a new sweetness, a graciousness of mien and movement absent before; Harunobu reduces them to captivating child-women, of flower-like fragility, but Koryūsai, Shigemasa and Kitao Masanobu gradually, with an increase in naturalism, give the figures nobler lines again, culminating in the queenly, Junoesque forms that Kiyonaga drew; while with Yeishi, Chōki and Utamaro,

Fig. 2. NISHIKAWA SUKENOBU: *Double-page from a picture-book of the occupations of women,* Yehon Tokiwa Gusa. 1731. (8½ × 13½ in.)

11

yet new, disturbing characteristics appear, the allure of languor and sophistication. The power to rise above the stereotyping that the Japanese system of tutelage tended to enforce, is the mark of the great artist.

A criticism often levelled at the Japanese print, or at Japanese painting generally for that matter, is that there is no characterization in the features, that all the faces look alike. Superficially, there is some truth in this; and the cause brings me back to my starting point, the distinction between Oriental and Occidental art. There was no *prima facie* obligation in the Japanese conception of painting to reproduce visual appearances: natural forms, of which the human head is one, were introduced into a picture with only as much realism as was compatible with the painter's objective: and so, the face, as an element in the design, received no more, and no less, attention than the other components in that design. Singling out the face for detailed treatment would have unbalanced the composition: in fact, their art, relying primarily on line without the Western device of chiaroscuro, tended to become caricatural when portraiture was attempted, as Sharaku's prints, with their greater realism, tend to prove.

But within these limits, there are evident differences between each great artist's depiction of the head: each had his own ideal, his work can be identified by his predilection for a certain facial type, as a study of the reproductions will show. For instance, however close in other respects the drawings of Harunobu, Buncho and Shunsho may have been at one period, there is no mistaking the small-featured demure face of Harunobu's *musume* for the aquiline, more experienced face of Buncho's, or the rounder, placid countenance favoured by Shunsho for either. Utamaro went even further, and proclaimed himself on a certain famous series of prints the 'Physiognomist', and although even these heads are far from satisfying our own ideas of portraiture, there is evident characterization of recognizable types: types, be it noted, rather than individuals: the general rather than the particular.

THE TECHNIQUE OF THE COLOUR-PRINT

The success of the illustrated book, and the demand by the common people for pictures that could be displayed, as in the upper-class houses, in the *tokonoma*, a quiet corner of a room where a picture could be contemplated with undisturbed serenity, led to the production of separate broadsheets, *ichimai-ye*, of larger size than the normal illustrated book. These broadsheets were at first in black outline only, but within a very short time, the need more closely to imitate paintings led to the application of colour by hand, and so the earliest Japanese print—not a true 'colour-print' at this stage—is in outline only, or roughly touched in with strong colours that match the forceful lines of the woodcut.

There is nothing more impressive in the whole range of Japanese art than the large prints of the great masters of this period, Moronobu, Kwaigetsudō, Sugimura, the first Kiyonobu, Kiyomasu and the young Okumura Masanobu. In their depictions of courtesan and paramour, actor and theatre-goer, there is the swing of an undulating line, a rhythmic flow in design and a boldness of contour admirably fitted to the woodcut line.

An additional refinement introduced during this period was the application of lustrous black and of brass and other metal dusts over a gum base in imitation of lacquer-work with applied gold. Known from this as 'lacquer-prints', *urishi-ye,* this kind of print is often of a barbaric splendour in its sombre colour and glinting brass-dust, and some supremely beautiful examples were designed by Kiyomasu, Okumura Masanobu and his pupil Toshinobu, and by Shigenaga.

The outline and hand-coloured prints prevailed for several decades, and it was not until about 1740 that colours as well as the outlines were printed from wood blocks, and even then, for another twenty years or so, the colours so applied were limited to two, usually a light red and a green. With the coming of the two-colour prints came a change in the designs, a tendency to smaller size, to slenderer figures, less robust decorative motifs: a change due, it seems likely, to the artists' unerring sense of balance, the feeling that the rose and green would be garish if applied to prints on the scale of the outline-prints that had hitherto prevailed.

Okumura Masanobu, one of the greatest of the 'primitives' and responsible for a number of innovations, is again one of the outstanding figures where the two-coloured prints (*beni-ye*) are concerned, but by this time numerous artists of merit were working in the Ukiyo-ye style, notably the second Kiyonobu; Kiyohiro, and Kiyomitsu; Shigenaga and Toyonobu. With these artists one notices a gradual introduction of fresh motives for the broadsheets, idyllic scenes in which exquisitely clothed figures move gracefully against a lightly-indicated background, the curve of a river, the cone of Fuji beyond the ricefields, the corner of a tea-house with a bamboo beside it.

This idyllic, consciously poetic element became all-pervading in the work of Ukiyo-ye artists, and was miraculously enhanced by the introduction in 1764, traditionally by Harunobu, of the full polychrome print, the true *nishiki-ye,* or brocade-print, as it was called. The accession of new technical resources, the incentive given by a public gradually more cultured and discerning, brought an immense response from the artists, and from Harunobu onwards (his great output in full colour was limited to the six years between 1764 and his death in 1770), there was a succession of artists of

Fig. 3. ISODA KORYŪSAI:
The toy sailing boat.
About 1772. (28½ × 4⅞ in.)

13

first rank: Koryūsai; Shigemasa and his pupils Kitao Masanobu and Masayoshi; Shunshō and his pupils Shunkō and Shunyei; Toyoharu; Kiyonaga and his followers, Shunchō, Shunzan and Shunman; Yeishi and his pupils Yeishō, Yeisui and Yeiri; Utamaro; Chōki; Sharaku; Hokusai and his pupils Hokkei and Gakutei; Toyohiro; Toyokuni and his pupils Kunimasa, Kuniyoshi and Kunisada; Hiroshige; Yeisen. This makes a formidable list of names, but some conception of the wealth of talent exerting itself in the field of the colour-print is obtained if it is realized that even this long list could be doubled by including names of other pupils and independent artists whose work, if rarer, is often of very high quality.

The colour-print was the result of the collaboration of four distinct people: the publisher, who commissioned the work and co-ordinated the operations of the other three concerned in its production; whose importance, consequently, cannot be over-rated—many of the finest prints are due to the enterprise and discernment of publishers like Tsutaya Jūsaburō and Yeijudō; the designer, with whom this book is most intimately concerned; the engraver; and the printer. To these, some would add a fifth, quite logically—the paper-maker: the superb texture and surface of the hand-made, mulberry-bark papers do much to enhance the bloom and soft radiance of the colours.

The woodcut medium came naturally to the Ukiyo-ye artists. There was already in existence a body of facsimile wood-engravers, long trained in the cutting of brush-drawn characters for the texts of books. To such engravers, the cutting of an outline block from a brush drawing supplied by the artist was a comparatively simple matter, and an extremely high standard of fidelity was normal. It is a matter of surprise that the application of colour by wood-blocks was so long deferred, for Chinese colour-prints of the Seventeenth Century, employing a wide range of colours, must have been known in Yedo. No doubt the need to keep the price within the reach of the humble Yedo folk was one of the factors responsible.

Fig. 4. SHUNSHŌ AND SHIGEMASA: *A double-page from the picture-book 'A Mirror of Rival Beauties'.* 1776. (8½ × 11½ in.)

A great deal depended on the craftsmen responsible for engraving and printing. The artist merely supplied the drawing on transparent paper and indicated the colours by painting them in on a 'pull' from the 'key-block', as the outline print was known. The engraver, pasting the drawing face-down on a block of hard wood like cherry (not on the 'end-grain' as has been customary in the West since Bewick's day, but on the 'plank' in the manner of

Dürer's engravers), cut around the lines with a knife, and by clearing the wood between his lines, left them in high relief. The ink having been rubbed on to the raised lines, proofing paper was placed over the block, pressure was applied by rubbing a twist of hemp over the back of the paper, and a proof of the engraver's facsimile of the artist's design thus secured.

Usually, the artist's original drawing was cut to pieces by the engraver in preparing the key-block, but a number of brush drawings for prints exist which seem to suggest that in some cases the engraving was made from a copy of the original design.

After the artist had indicated the colours on a proof of the key-block, a separate block had to be cut for each colour that was to be printed, and in a print of complex tints, as many as ten or more such additional blocks might be required, from which, with over-printings, a remarkable range of colour was obtainable. The col-

Fig. 5. TORII KIYONAGA: *Autumn moon on the Sumida river*. Part of a five-sheet print. About 1787. (14¾ × 10 in.)

ours were mixed by the printer on each block separately, a little size made from rice being added to give a firm consistency. Accuracy of register, of first importance as a print passed from one block to another to receive its succession of colours, was secured by a guide-mark for the proofer, consisting of a right-angle cut at one corner of each block and a straight line at the opposite side, aligned with one side of the right-angle.

Until the Nineteenth Century, the colours were mainly of vegetable origin, and, unfortunately, fugitive on exposure to light, the sky-blue, violet and pink fading to buffs and greys still beautiful in themselves, but something quite different from the bright hues that originally caught the eye of the Yedo purchaser. With the singular perversity of their race, some collectors have affected to admire the time-faded print in preference to another in its original colours, but although many fade in harmony, the quiet, subdued tones of such prints are those of preserved flowers, lacking the gaiety and liveliness of the living thing. Besides, quite often the precious harmony of colour achieved by some artists, Harunobu in particular, is destroyed when more stable greens, yellows and a chocolate brown remain unimpaired whilst other shades have become uniformly dulled. To collectors of the kind mentioned, the print in its original state comes as much of a shock as cleaned pictures, seen at last in all their bright colour, come to lovers of the 'embrowned' tones of the Old Masters.

15

Among the various embellishing devices used by the printer are the use of mica in backgrounds, or for picking out mirrors and frosty or icy surfaces; the application of metal-dusts, either sprinkled or applied by block; and *gauffrage,* or blind-printing, for indicating the patterns and folds of dresses, the plumage of birds or the fur of animals, by lines in relief but without colour.

There seems to be no certainty as to the number of prints taken from one set of blocks, but an extant letter of Hokusai's to one of his publishers sets the limit at 200 prints, since, before that number is reached, the saturated block ceases to take the colour, and begins to wear down.

From a variety of causes, the sizes and shapes of the prints were constantly changing, but only the formats peculiar to the Japanese print need be mentioned. As a substitute for paintings, it was natural that quite early the *kakemono-ye* should have been introduced, since this most nearly resembled the hanging painting, and it was, in fact, often mounted like a painting on rollers. The diptych, triptych and other multi-sheet prints seem to have had their origin in the practice, prevalent among painters of the established schools, of producing two or three separate paintings that were linked partly by similarity of subject, partly by some underlying abstract theme, its roots, perhaps, in the teaching of the Zen sect of Buddhism, and beyond the reach of the unaided eye. But the colour-print triptychs, beginning in the Primitive period as three related figures printed adjacent to one another on a single sheet of paper (and usually cut into three by the owner), led to the diptych and triptych of Kiyonaga's time onward, in which the whole design was carried over two or three sheets which were intended to be joined at their edges, though, by a remarkable feat of designing, each sheet can be enjoyed as an independent entity, with no disturbing sensation that companion sheets are lacking to complete the picture.

Though uncommon, prints were produced comprising five sheets or more, and these more nearly correspond to the *makemono* or laterally-rolled painting. It was more often intended, I think, that these panoramic prints should be viewed, not as a single composition but piecemeal, a few sheets at a time, just as the old *makemono* was unrolled to reveal only as much as the eye could take in at a glance.

Surimono (literally 'printed-things') were prints issued for some specific occasion, as New Year's greetings, to celebrate a birth or a marriage, to commemorate a new membership to a poetry club, or to give notice of an author's or artist's change of name, no rare event. They are usually of small size and characterized by the extreme delicacy of the printing, the lavish use of metal dusts and gauffrage, and the welding of design and poetry into a decorative whole. Shunman, Hokusai and his pupils Hokkei, Shinsai and Gakutei, excelled in these miniature works of art, which sometimes seem to trespass into the realm of the lacquerer.

The *hashirakake,* 'pillar-hanging' print, is, of all the formats used by the designers, the most essentially Japanese, and without a counterpart in Western art.

16

Intended as a decoration for the wooden pillars that were a feature of the lightly-constructed houses of the country, the difficulties of designing within the tall, narrow limits of the panel seem to have challenged the Ukiyo-ye artists to some of their finest achievements, comparable to the way that the limitation to seventeen syllables, all that the favourite form of lyric permitted, inspired the poets to remarkable feats of expressive compression. Harunobu, and especially Koryūsai, are the great masters of the *hashirakake*, but Kiyonaga, Yeishi, Utamaro and most of the outstanding artists of the latter end of the Eighteenth Century produced fine prints of this kind.

THE PRINT-SELLERS' PUBLIC

The colour-print's appeal to us is only in part due to the actual style of the Ukiyo-ye school: it resides as much in the portrayal of a world utterly remote from our own, with dress, behaviour and custom intensely national, or influenced only from a quarter equally remote from us, China. It is this fusion of alien subject and individual style that makes the colour-print far more a national art, a 'folk' art if you will, than say, Italian painting, however distinctive the latter may seem in relation to other European styles.

Fig. 6. KATSUKAWA SHUNSHŌ: *The actor Danjuro V in character.* About 1780. (10 × 5 in.)

The formation of the new social class has already been touched upon as being the genesis of the colour-print. The character of the people of this plebeian class, their customs and daily life, their culture, have an intimate bearing on the nature of the prints.

Geographically, the Japanese are an isolated race. This insularity was accentuated in 1638, at a time when the Tokugawa regime was fully established, by laws proscribing intercourse with countries outside Japan; a policy that had its strength in that it preserved the country from distracting foreign influences, in the way of modern totalitarianism; and its weaknesses, that came from denying the people the broadening influence of other ways of life, other philosophies, than their own, and of the benefits, albeit sometimes doubtful, of scientific progress being made elsewhere. But in respect of their art, the effect of the seclusion was

17

wholly good, if one is to judge by the Europeanization that, after the revolution of 1868, ensued with results completely disastrous to the national genius.

But just as in-breeding leads to certain perversions and degenerate types, so in the Japan of this period there is something febrile and unbalanced, it is a world of rigid etiquette and extreme fastidiousness in dress, where, quite apart from the drama, men are often posed in feminine attire; and yet a world of the utmost grossness and brutality, where self-immolation is decreed for a peccadillo, and any crime sanctioned in the cause of revenge.

Too great a stress has often been placed, I think, on the low station and vulgar taste of the people to whom the prints were purveyed. From the very nature of many of the prints, the refinement of the sentiment expressed, the artist's evident familiarity with classic poetry, it is obvious that they were acquired by people whose tastes were anything but coarse. There is a likeness here—it has been remarked before—between the people of Elizabethan England and the Japanese of the Yedo period; we are constantly surprised at the richness of allusion in Shakespeare, which modern editors need copious commentaries to explain, but which was matter of everyday knowledge to the frequenters of the 'Globe'.

The Eighteenth Century saw, in fact, not only the increase in the literacy of those of lowest station, but also an intermingling of the military and controlling class with the wealthier merchants, considered very low in the social scale, and inter-marriage between such disparates, unthinkable earlier, also helped to break down the former rigid barriers. It is well known that the *Kabuki* Theatre, though considered an amusement for the lower classes, was, even if only clandestinely, frequented by the two-sworded men, the *samurai*, and we may be sure that many of the prints, and the finest of the illustrated books, were intended for the same exalted class. In a book of Hokusai's, 'The Pleasures of Yedo', 1802, there is a picture of the print-shop of Tsutaya Jūsaburō, one of the leading publishers of the day, with a *samurai* standing at the counter and showing a marked interest in the colour-prints; and a picture of a *samurai* seated in another publisher's shop, engrossed in one of the Ukiyo-ye picture books, appears in a book of 1801 illustrated by Toyokuni. The work of Harunobu, Yeishi, Utamaro, and Shunman, to cite only four, is often of that hyper-refinement termed by the Japanese *shibui*, and would assuredly have been quite lost on the vulgar herd.

But that there were extremes in the vast populace of Yedo is not to be doubted, and the literature of the time, which, like the arts of the lacquerer and the potter, the silk-weaver and the painter, received new impetus and created new forms in the dynamic atmosphere of the period, ranges from moral and religious treatises of the *Kangakusha*, the enthusiasts for all things Chinese, to *kibyoshi*, 'yellow-backs' and fiction of various kinds, often of a pornographic type. Of this literature, by which some judgement of the taste and mental calibre of the people can be made, W. G. Aston wrote, 'But while the new literature is much richer and of a more vigorous growth than the old, there is a sad falling off in the point of form . . . Extravagance, false sentiment, defiance of probability, whether physical or

18

moral, pedantry, pornography, puns and meretricious ornaments of style, intolerable platitudes, impossible adventures and weary wastes of useless detail meet us everywhere'.

As might be expected, the Ukiyo-ye artists, as regards the subject-matter of their prints, can often be taxed with similar faults, but generally, certainly until the decline of the art in the Nineteenth Century, the age-old traditions of draughtsmanship and design still exerted a powerful influence, not lessened by affiliation to the new school. As an instance, one might take the books of erotic pictures. Practically every artist was responsible for books of this nature, books which were half-heartedly banned from time to time, but usually only slightly frowned upon by the authorities: but even in these the artists never forsook their high principles of drawing and composition, and, in fact, artists like Yeishi and Utamaro seemed to find fresh access of powers in grappling with the problems set by imbroglios of semi-nude figures, and some of their finest designs, reproduced by the most sumptuous colour-printing, are to be found in these *shungwa*, 'Spring-drawings', as the erotic pictures are called.

Judged by their literature, and by the majority of the prints and picture-books, the commoners and their more aristocratic congeners were obsessed with a love of the gay, the fast, life: modern Japanese, in fact, translate the word *Ukiyo-ye* as 'Pictures of Gay Life'. Prints and books are replete with pictures of pleasure-parties in the town, the countryside or along the river, the youth of both sexes freely intermingling and philandering, to the accompaniment often of music, and with the *sake*-kettle always ready to hand. The Yoshiwara, the brothel quarter, was a constant pre-occupation of the Ukiyo-ye artists, and the *Kabuki* theatre provided almost as many subjects. These, with *kwachō* (pictures of birds and flowers), and landscape, a later, Nineteenth-Century development, form the subject matter of the prints, a little more detailed consideration of which is an aid to appreciating the nature of the people, and the art of the print-designers.

THE COURTESAN AND THE 'GAY LIFE'

The courtesan was, in all senses of the word, a public figure. Accepted by the authorities as an inevitable feature of town life—the large numbers of officials quartered in Yedo without their families, and the lack of romance in the pre-

Fig. 7.
KATSUKAWA SHUNCHŌ:
Girl by the Sacred Pine.
About 1789. ($27\frac{1}{4} \times 4\frac{7}{8}$ in.)

19

arranged marriage of the country were partial causes—the Yoshiwara in Yedo and similar establishments elsewhere were set apart for licensed prostitution. The Yoshiwara became the haunt of most of the artists and writers of the time in search of 'copy', for the town-dwellers were always avid for pictures of the 'Green-Houses', of the colourful life of this world-within-a-world, and especially for portraits of the denizens, the courtesans, from the *taiyū*, the queen of her calling, and the *ōiran*, the next in the heirarchy, down to the acolytes of the profession, the *shinzō* and *kamuro*.

The higher-class courtesans, destined for those of high rank or great wealth, were trained from children to become fit consorts for such men. They bore themselves like princesses, whose accomplishments they emulated, learning to speak the ancient poetic language, practising the arts of music, painting and poetry, and carrying themselves in their gorgeous apparel with regal grace.

Various factors led to their popularity with the colour-print artists, apart from the public demand for pictures of the reigning beauties. Though these were never portraits in our sense of the term, they were unquestionably fashion-plates, and to a nation such as the Japanese, where both men and women were absorbed in matters of dress, the patterns and colours of silks, this was a major attraction. In a celebrated book of 1776, entitled 'A Mirror of Beauties of the Green-Houses', illustrated by Shigemasa and Shunshō, the publisher, Tsutaya Jūsaburō, calls attention in a preface to the Japanese artists' preoccupation with 'the fashions of costume and hair-dressing prevalent at each age, which pass as rapidly as the infant growing to manhood'; and from Moronobu onwards, the changes in dress fashions, in the motifs of the silk-designers, but especially the alterations in coiffure styles, are marked enough to date the prints with some reliability. The features of a girl's face often seemed of less concern to the artist than the set of her hair, the drawing of which, with its complement of combs, was always given in considerable detail. One could easily believe that with the Japanese the hair was in truth 'a woman's crowning glory', and the beautiful, and often eccentric, shapes into which it was forced, play a large part in the pattern of the print-designers' compositions.

But the sway of fashion in Japan was not limited to dress or coiffure: the prints give clear evidence of the vogue of certain physical types: the tall, majestic figure of the Primitives giving way gradually to the improbable *petite* of Harunobu, and this to the immensely tall and slim forms affected by Kiyonaga, Yeishi and Utamaro. In the artists' drawings, there was rarely any truth to the actual Japanese feminine form: in this again the artists showed their complete independence of the dictates of nature. The actual build of the average Japanese woman was, and is, short and a little dumpy, but this did not prevent the artists from imparting to their models the ample majesty of the Parthenon 'Fates', or the dainty sprightliness of Watteau's shepherdesses, or the willowy grace of Modigliani's attenuated creatures: all in accordance with the canon of proportions dictated by the leaders of fashion.

20

Fig. 8. KITIGAWA UTAMARO: *Cicada and snail with fruit and plants.* A double-page from the 'Insect Book'. 1788. (10 × 15 in.)

The 'Pleasures of Yedo' is the title on scores of colour-print books and on a multitude of prints. Usually, they depict the gallants escorting courtesans and their more virtuous associates, the geishas, in the well-known thoroughfares of the town, making their way to a popular rendezvous, tea-house or theatre; or in pleasure-boats on the Sumida river, the favourite setting for trifling amours and mild debauchery; or in the lovely gardens abounding in the purlieus of Yedo, rapt in admiration of the flowering cherry trees, perhaps, or of the red maple leaves floating on a pool.

The town of Yedo, itself like a huge pleasure-garden with impermanent-looking houses and bridges of fanciful shape spanning the river, was often *en fête*. Each month had its own festival celebrated with spectacular processions and pageantry, regattas on the river and firework displays, providing the Ukiyo-ye artists with wonderful opportunities for compositions crowded with figures in flamboyant costumes, and alive with the gaiety and abandon of carnival.

At other times, we are given glimpses of the interiors of the Yoshiwara apartments, of the ceremonial of the 'courtship' preceding 'full knowledge'. Or the women are seen alone, idling the day away in decorous pursuits, writing long love-letters, displaying a new dress to companions, amusing themselves with pet animals, or with battledore or yo-yo.

As the Eighteenth Century waned, there were other reasons for the popularity of the Yoshiwara among the artists and intellectuals generally. The unrest in the

21

country caused by the ferment against the Shogunate led to repressive measures, and many of the men who sowed the seed that came to fruition in the revolution of 1868 found sanctuary in the precincts of the Yoshiwara, which became a cloak for the 'underground' movement, a place where freedom of thought and speech was possible despite harsh laws. In the luxuriously appointed quarters of the Yoshiwara, literary wits of the time like Kitao Masanobu and Jippensha Ikku (themselves both designers of prints), Utamaro, Toyokuni and their fellow artists, rubbed shoulders with the political firebrands seeking refuge there, and something of the charged atmosphere, the undercurrent of violence beneath the froth and sparkle of wit, gives the prints of the late Nineteenth Century a strangely disturbing character, a sort of *fin-de-siècle* sophistication new to Japanese art.

THE THEATRE

The theatre was, to the Yedo commoner, all part of the 'Gay Life'. It was recorded assiduously by the Ukiyo-ye artists, and some of the finest prints of the school are of actors in character.

The *Kabuki* theatre originated in the Seventeenth Century, only a few decades before the Ukiyo-ye school began to find its outlet in the illustration of books. It was a composite, combining features from the old dances of Japan, from the classical Nō drama of the aristocracy, and from the already popular puppet stage. The *Kabuki* was a typical product of the new class: the stiff brocade and ritualistic dance of the Nō plays were replaced by fashionable silk and greater freedom of movement, the recondite acted poetry gave way to something more nearly approaching realism in speech and action, even though to our intelligence both are still mannered and non-naturalistic. The art of the *Kabuki* theatre was as much visual as literary, partaking in some degree of the character of our ballet, though the movements were more restricted, the drama more intense, and the tempo so slow that at times the stage seemed to present a series of colourful tableaux. The plays were sanguinary, full of violence, heroics and bathotic situations, and hardly stand high as literature, but they provided magnificent material for the colour-print designers, certain sub-schools coming into being primarily as recorders of stage performances and as portrait-makers of the actors.

Most Ukiyo-ye artists at one time or another took the stage as their subject, but to two families of artists in particular we are indebted for the finest work in this sphere: the Torii, of whom Kiyonobu, Kiyomasu, Kiyohiro, Kiyomitsu and Kiyonaga are the great masters; and the Katsukawa, Shunshō and his pupils Shunkō and Shunyei and others less well known.

In their prints, little attempt is made to give the scene of a play, a few unobtrusive 'props' being all that was required to set the stage for the fanatical theatre-goers. Normally, the prints depict either a single actor, or less often, two, in character, and from Kiyonobu onwards, the artists show a wonderful ingenuity

22

in composing a rhythmic design based on a single figure, or two in a sort of *pas-de-deux*. As on the Elizabethan stage, only male performers were permitted, but certain families of actors specialised in female parts, and judging by the prints, their impersonations seem to have been deceptively life-like. Few can resist the charm of the 'girl' in the flowered straw hat in Okumura Masanobu's print (Plate 7) and it is hard to believe that the model for such feminine grace of movement was a male actor.

Shunshō is perhaps the greatest master of the actor-print, and at his best delights us with the dancing arabesque of his figures against a slightly indicated back-drop, using a simple outline and flat tones of soft harmonious colouring. Yet, despite the absence of what we call realism, he gives us a convincing picture of the actors of the Yedo theatres. One Western writer, Mr. Osman Edwards, familiar with the *Kabuki* performances, wrote, 'To watch act after act of their spectacular tragedies is like looking through a portfolio of their best colour-prints'.

The prints of Sharaku need special mention, because although founded in the tradition of the theatrical colour-print, they have qualities that distinguish them at once from all other prints of the same order. The intensity of characterization, the forcible draughtsmanship, the bizarre and sinister harmonies of colour, accentuated by the dark mica-grounds of most, compel attention even when they disturb or even revolt us. The staring eyeballs, the unnatural grimace, are no more than an interpretation of the intensity of expression affected by the actors, though in some of the prints there are, I think, the marks of a would-be master who, like Cézanne sometimes, has to struggle to express himself, hampered and angered by the limitations of his draughtsmanship. Perhaps the most astonishing thing to relate in connection with Sharaku's prints, not unconnected with this sense of a giant wrestling with an intractable medium, is that they were all produced in one year, 1794, and that there is no evidence to show that the artist, a Nō dancer by profession, had ever designed a colour-print before that date.

KWACHŌ AND LANDSCAPE

From earliest times, the Japanese people were united in an unfeigned devotion to nature. Literature, legend, painting, ceramic and textile all bear testimony to an innate love of flowers and trees, birds and animals, and all the natural features of the countryside. The rising of the new moon was celebrated by gatherings who composed lyrics as they watched the sky; the flowering of the cherry-trees was made the occasion for 'viewing-parties', the red leaves of the autumn maples, and the first falls of snow, brought admiring groups into the countryside; the mountains and lakes of their beautiful land were literally worshipped—who can forget the picture in Hokusai's book 'The One-hundred Views of Fuji' of an old man kneeling before a circular window framing a distant view of Fuji and flinging back his head in an ecstasy of delight at the vision? Poems extolling the Peerless

Mountain, Lake Biwa and the lesser known features of every province, are legion.

In art, this deep feeling for nature gave rise to a pure landscape art long before such a thing appeared in European painting, and also, to paintings of 'birds and flowers', *Kwachō*, that really have no counterpart in our art at all. The greatest painters of the Kano and Chinese schools excelled in paintings of these two kinds, and their works were revered with something next to idolatry, the finest resting in the temples as objects of devotion.

As will be mentioned shortly, the Ukiyo-ye artists were inclined to deal in a rather cavalier manner with the subjects hallowed by antiquity and traditionally associated with the aristocratic schools of painting, but in their landscape and *kwachō* art, though still unmistakably Ukiyo-ye in timbre, the note is often of great sincerity, and the humble prints challenge comparison with the paintings of Sesshū and Motonobu, Sō-ami and Chokuan, and other giants of the past.

There are early *kwachō* from the hands of such primitives as Kiyomasu, Shigenaga and others, whose drawings of hawks, for instance, in striking black line only, are often of an impressive magniloquence: but Harunobu and Koryūsai, Utamaro, Hokusai and Hiroshige, with the greater resources of the colour-print proper at their command, excelled in this field, producing exquisite designs of birds and animals that exemplify the astonishing power of the Japanese to synthesize and conventionalize natural forms, to bring them into an ordered pattern, without destroying the illusion of life, of actuality.

The art of the popular school was primarily in *genre* painting, manners and modes of the ordinary life of the day, and from the earliest book illustrations it was habitual to set the scene with a glimpse of tree or stream, the outline of tea-house or Yoshiwara, in the background. However, landscape, as an independent art, appeared late in the prints, though Toyoharu with his Europeanized *Uki-ye* 'bird's-eye-view' prints may be an exception to the rule. By the time of Kiyonaga, Yeishi and Utamaro, the background was often given greater prominence, and in their *plein air* pictures, the pleasure-gardens, the streets of Yedo, the river-front, are effectively sketched in. Utamaro, in some albums of about 1790, produced some prints that are pure landscape, but it was left to Hokusai and Hiro-

Fig. 9. HOKUSAI: *Page from the picture-book 'One hundred Views of the Fuji'*. 1835. (8 × 5½ in.)

24

shige to develop this last achievement of the colour-print art, one that, with our natural bias towards landscape art, delights us more spontaneously than any other.

Hokusai's landscape prints, though based on the age-old traditions, are daringly innovating, and owe much of their *éclat* to the colour-print technique. This medium, imposing broad treatment, firm outline and flat washes of colour, seemed to inspire him to design in a synoptic manner, disdaining the accidents of topography and weather the better to achieve the essential hill, the eternal sea: though, in the true Ukiyo-ye vein, it is only rarely that man is absent, dwarfed and intimidated though he may be by the elemental forces and forms around him.

Fig. 10. GAKUTEI: *Carp leaping a water-fall.* About 1840. (8 × 7 in.)

Hiroshige is a milder and gentler spirit altogether, the figures, the human element, loom larger in the foreground, and generally we feel that we are in a land where rain and moonlight are much as they are with us. Our sympathies are won over not only by his artistry, but by the sense that, though essentially Japanese, he is in some indefinable way closer to us, in style and sentiment, than any of his forerunners, and his brush-drawings bring this out, if anything, more clearly.

LEGEND AND HISTORY

It is testimony to that strange duality in the life of the Japanese to which reference has already been made, the indulgence in all forms of sensuous pleasure and an ardent appreciation of the arts against a background of violence, fanatical loyalty and revenge, to us wholly barbaric, that the Ukiyo-ye artists often turned from the blandishments of the 'Green-Houses' and the theatre to subjects from heroic legends, and particularly from the bloody events of mediaeval history, barely distinguishable themselves in the passage of time from the most improbable of the legends.

Chief among these legendary histories, or historical romances, are those dealing with the civil wars of the middle ages between the two dominant clans, the Minamoto and Taira. The stirring events of these wars, the great battles and the individual feats of chivalry and derring-do recur again and again, few artists being able to resist this type of print, perhaps because an innate nationalistic pride in the past led to the unfailing popularity with the public of such depictions. Even those artists whose charm lies in an essentially feminine grace, Harunobu, for instance, or Shunzan, became changed spirits as they buckled on the cumbrous old armour and turned manfully to the warlike themes, the fight on Gojo Bridge, for example, between Yoshitsune and the giant Benkei—a favourite subject—or Hachimantaro, heroic youth of the Minamoto clan, performing prodigies of valour.

But the great master of these scenes of strife is unquestionably Kuniyoshi, who, in the mid-19th century, produced a great number of powerful designs, many of them in triptych form, that convey a sense of turbulence and pageantry that has a reality of its own, whatever relation it may bear to historical fact.

PARODY, TRAVESTY, BURLESQUE AND ANALOGUE

The newcomer to Ukiyo-ye art will often be puzzled by the artists' oblique manner of illustrating a given theme, and by the even less straightforward manner of entitling prints. Subjects reverently painted by artists of the established schools are whimsically enacted by courtesan and paramour in 'modern dress'; and going further, by an odd transmogrification, classical landscapes and famous views are personified by women of the Green-Houses, whose trivial occupations are ingeniously made to suggest, by remote analogy, famous places and events, and the classical painters' representations of them.

The Seven Famous Scenes in the life of the poetess Komachi were handled in this way by nearly every Ukiyo-ye artist of note: a mother and child, for instance, looking in a mirror, are made to do service for the 'Komachi and the Parrot' scene, the pun-loving Japanese seeing an immediate connection between the 'Echo-poem' returned by Komachi to the Emperor Yosai, using all the same characters save one that comprised his own poem, and the two reflected faces in the mirror. Even more popular was the linking of the traditional 'Eight Views of Lake Biwa' with scenes in domestic life: in the print of Koryūsai's reproduced, the two girls playing with a toy boat in a basin represent a typical Ukiyo-ye perversion of the 'Return of Sailing-boats to Yabase'. Other favourite subjects with the Kano painters, the jolly madman Kanzan and Jitoku, traditionally shown as ragamuffin figures, one with a scroll, the other with a besom broom, are represented by girls attired *à la mode*, a love-letter taking the place of the scroll, and as often as not, a guitar serving for the besom. The six famous 'jewel-rivers' of Japan were invariably personified by gorgeously apparelled women of the Yoshiwara, some pattern of their robe or some action whose significance may be lost upon us, giving the locality of each river.

Parody and travesty are hardly exact words for this sort of thing, though occasionally the playful treatment of well-known stories or legends amounts almost to burlesque: as for example, the enactment of the Tenth-Century court scenes from the Genji Romance by fashionable ladies of the demi-monde, and the representation of scenes from the popular melodrama 'The Forty-Seven Rōnin' by pictures of domestic squabble or low-life courtship, far-fetched parallels to which a clue was often given by a small inset drawing of the actual scene burlesqued.

THE ART OF UKIYO-YE

The study of a piece of music, a *lied* of Hugo Wolf's for example, an analysis of the score and a translation of the lyric, brings us only a little way towards an appreciation of the musician's art, which lies in the fusion of words and accompaniment, and can be judged by the sounds alone. Having glanced at the environment of the Ukiyo-ye artists, the class of people for whom their art came into being, the technique and the subject-matter of the prints, there is still something to be added concerning the especial aesthetic appeal of the prints, an appeal as difficult to translate into words as that of rhythm, melody and counterpoint. Primarily, it is a matter of pure design, of the fusion of line and colour, subject and composition, into 'pictorial music', addressed to our sight as the *lied* is to our hearing.

Of the pictorial art of few other nations can it be said that it compares with that of the Japanese print-designers in so nearly achieving that aspiration towards a 'condition of music', tardily accepted in Europe as the ultimate aim of graphic art. A knowledge of the language, customs, history, literature and legends of the country may in some cases aid our appreciation, but at other times may actually interfere with the more purely emotional acceptance of the print as a work of art, returning a magic amalgam into its separate components.

Founded, for all its revolutionary character, in a tradition of painting that had never adopted mere representationalism as one of its tenets, and aided by a medium that inhibited any tendency to elaborate beyond firm outlines and flat tones of colour, the art of the Ukiyo-ye artists stands or falls ultimately on an assessment of its design: and there are many who will agree with Laurence Binyon and O'Brien Sexton whose considered opinion was that 'As pure design, this body of work is unrivalled in any other country, unless perhaps by Greek vases'.

Given a space to fill, the Japanese designers seem to have had an innate gift for decorating it in a manner felt by us to be inevitable. This is brought home most clearly, perhaps, in the Kwachō of Harunobu, Koryusai, Utamaro and Hokusai, in which the shapes and colours of bird and flower are brought with masterly skill into compositions that satisfy us like rounded melodies, and are unerringly given the perfect *mise-en-page*. In the process, just as the faces of the courtesans are reduced in other prints to a few expressive lines, the minutiae of fur and feather may be sacrificed, and botanically the flowers might not convince Bentham and Hooker: but the drawings bring out the essentials, the plant really seems to be growing, the bird is unmistakably alive and capable of flight.

But this genius for synthesis is not limited to their designs for kwachō: its greatest triumphs were in the drawing of the human form. 'Art is first of all unity of impression' wrote Fenollosa, 'but into this unity can be thrown and melted every serviceable form that generous nature can supply'. In the figure designs, comprising by far the greater proportion of the prints, there is the same reduction to essentials, the same insistence on pattern. The relation of figure to figure may

27

seem accidental, the pose of each naturalistic, but in reality, the arrangements are quite artificial, as much bent to the artist's will as the artfully placed spray of flowers or the bird on the wing.

In landscape, too, the utmost ingenuity and invention are brought to bear in composition. Hokusai is undoubtedly supreme in this power of reducing the disorder of nature to a formal pattern that still has the impress of actuality and is never mere conventionalized form. The series of forty-six prints entitled 'The Thirty-six Views of Mount Fuji', the cone-shaped mountain appearing in each print like a *leit-motif*, is a display of virtuosity akin to the Diabelli Variations of Beethoven: and for daring composition even these are excelled by the series of 'Waterfalls'. Hiroshige combines a faculty for pictorial pattern with great use of the unusual viewpoint. The snow-covered fields around Yedo are seen from a great height with the eyes of an eagle, whose outspread wings fill the upper part of the design; the Iris Gardens of Horikiri are glimpsed through the irises themselves, brought close to the viewer's eyes; the bow-moon, in a famous print, is seen low down in the sky between precipitous cliffs that soar to each side of the panel.

In these achievements of the figure-designers and landscapists in the realm of composition, their sacrifice of detail and bold synthesis of natural forms, their adoption of the unusual angle or view-point in the cause of a telling design, in all this there may seem little that is novel to us today. But the impact and effect on European art in the Nineteenth Century cannot be over-estimated. The growth during the century among European artists of the conception of an art based on, rather than tied to, nature, the breaking away from the dogma of representing 'things as they are seen', was due indirectly to the lesson of the East: and many painters were directly influenced by the design of the Ukiyo-ye artists, their manner of employing human form and landscape feature as elements of a pictorial pattern. Degas, Manet, Van Gogh, Toulouse-Lautrec, Beardsley, the Beggarstaff Brothers —to take a number of artists at random—all show indebtedness at one phase or another of their work to the designers of the Japanese colour-prints.

By a sad turning of the tables, the influence of Western art on the Japanese was to cause first a flirting with, then a complete subjection to, the very representational method already, by their example, discredited in the West. Watercolour was forsaken for oil-paint, quite inimical to their native technique, and the traditional styles of painting that had prevailed for centuries and given rise to a body of painting unique in character, were thrown over for imitations of European methods, mostly of a debased 'photographic' type.

But the influence of alien models can hardly be held to account for the deterioration in the art of the Ukiyo-ye school. Even before the country was opened up to foreigners in 1853, in fact from the beginning of the century, there were signs of a falling off from the high standards that had prevailed until then, and the broadsheets, issued now in vast numbers for an increasingly uncritical public, gradually became poorer in the quality both of the designs and of the colour-printing.

28

Fig. 11. YEISEN: *Inagawa Bridge, Nojiri*. About 1840. ($8\frac{7}{8} \times 13\frac{5}{8}$ in.)

Hokusai and certain of his pupils; Hiroshige; Kuniyoshi, and, for a time, Kunisada continued to produce fine prints, despite the evil effect on the colour-printing caused by the replacement of vegetable colours by aniline dyes of foreign manufacture; but by the time of the Revolution of 1868, the art of the Ukiyo-ye colour-print was dead. There were attempts to revive the art later in the century, and the engravers, at least, showed that they had not forgotten their craft: but the designers' art had been finally vitiated by contact with the West, and few of the later prints rise above either ineffectual prettiness, or violently coloured melodrama.

Fig. 12. HIROSHIGE: *Chrysanthemums and a* kakemono *depicting a full moon.*
Fan-mount. About 1835–40. ($8\frac{5}{8} \times 11\frac{3}{8}$ in.)

PLATES

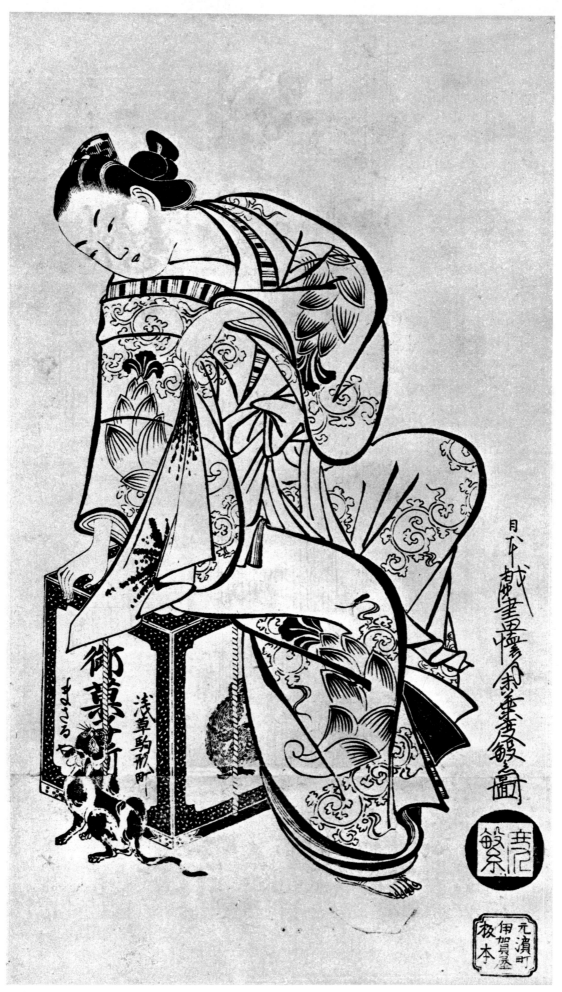

1. KWAIGETSUDŌ DOHAN : *Courtesan playing with a cat*. About 1710. Ink-print (*sumi-ye*). (21⅞ × 12¼ in.)

2. HISHIKAWA MORONOBU: *Returning from a flower-picnic*. About 1675. Unsigned ink-print, hand-coloured. (10½ × 16⅜ in.)

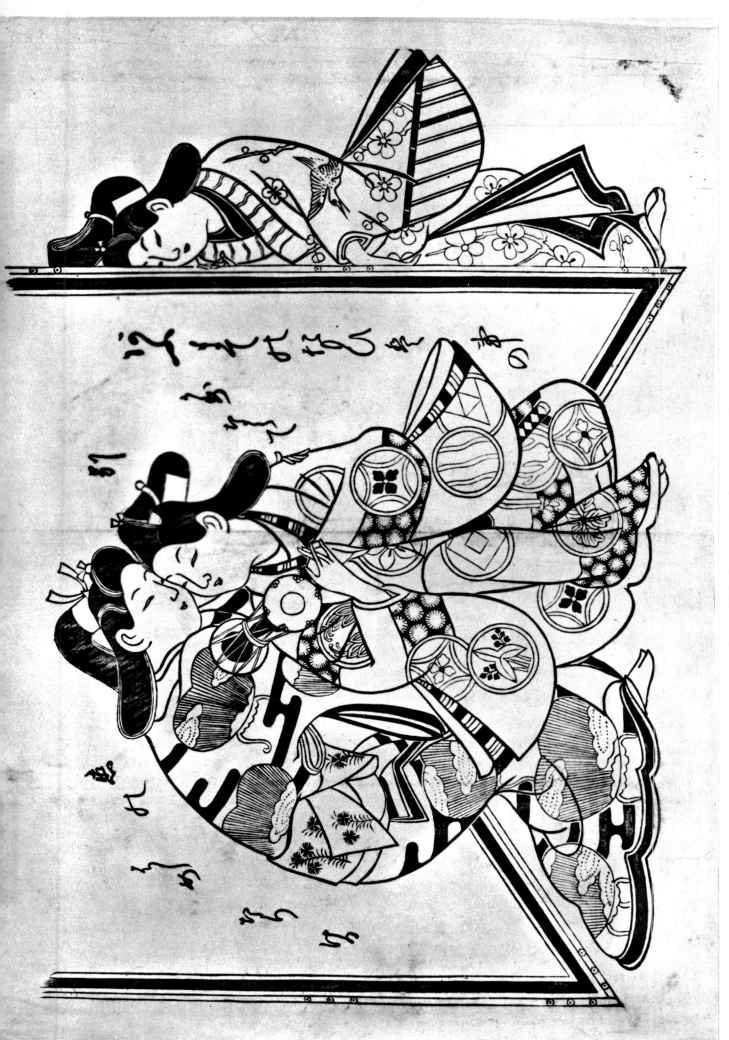

3. SUGIMURA JIHEI: *Lovers discovered behind a screen*. About 1690. A page from an album. (14½ × 10⅝ in.)

4. TORII KIYONOBU I: *Two actors in the play called 'Saya-ate'*. About 1700. Ink-print. (10¼ × 5¾ in.)

小野小町
嵐 之 丸

鳥居清倍筆

5. TORII KIYOMASU I: *Arashi Wakano as the poetess Ono no Komachi, dancing*. About 1715. Hand-coloured lacquer print. $(10\frac{3}{4} \times 6\frac{1}{8}$ in.)

6. Okumura Masanobu: *Courtesan*. About 1705. (16¾ × 11½ in.)

7. OKUMURA MASANOBU : *An actor as a girl dancing.* About 1715. (12 × 8½ in.)

8. NISHIMURA SHIGENAGA: *The actor Sanjo Kantarō as a tea-seller*. About 1725. Hand-coloured lacquer print. (13 × 6¼ in.)

9. TORII KIYOHIRO: *Children spinning tops*. About 1745. Print in green and rose. ($17 \times 11\frac{7}{8}$ in.)

10. OKUMURA TOSHINOBU: *Actors as a flower-seller and a street musician.* About 1740. Hand-coloured lacquer print. (13 × 6¼ in.)

11a. Ishikawa Toyonobu: *A Korean Envoy*. About 1740. Hand-coloured ink-print. (26¼×6 in.)

11b. Ishikawa Toyonobu: *Girl closing an umbrella*. About 1760. Print in three colours. (26½×4¼ in.)

12. OKUMURA MASANOBU: *The Love-Letter*. About 1748. Hand-coloured print. (24×9¾ in.)

尾上菊五郎

鳥居清倍筆

13. KIYOMASU II : *The actor Onoye Kikujoro as a courtier dancing.* About 1745. Print in green and rose. (11⅞ × 5½ in.)

14. ISHIKAWA TOYONOBU: *Boy dancing with a hobby-horse*. About 1755. Print in green and rose. (17 × 12 in.)

15. Torii Kiyomitsu: *Actors as lovers in a play*. 1765. Print in three colours. ($17\frac{1}{4} \times 12\frac{1}{8}$ in.)

16. Suzuki Harunobu: *The Summer Shower*. 1765.

17a. Suzuki Harunobu: *A courtesan looking at the moon's reflection*. About 1768. $(27 \times 4\frac{1}{2}$ in.)

17b. Suzuki Harunobu: *Lovers sharing an umbrella*. About 1770. $(26\frac{1}{2} \times 4\frac{7}{8}$ in.)

18. SUZUKI HARUNOBU: *The Sacred White Horse.* About 1767. ($10\frac{7}{8} \times 8\frac{1}{4}$ in.)

19. SUZUKI HARUNOBU : *Girls fording a stream*. About 1766. Unsigned. ($9\frac{3}{4} \times 7\frac{1}{8}$ in.)

20. ISODA KORYŪSAI: *The courtesan Morokoshi of Echizenya*. About 1775. (15¼ × 10 in.)

21. ISODA KORYŪSAI: *Man and girl on the verandah of a house*. About 1772. (10 × 7¼ in.)

22. ISODA KORYŪSAI : *Feeding carp*. Unsigned. About 1771. ($9\frac{3}{4} \times 7\frac{1}{2}$ in.)

23. ISODA KORYŪSAI: Rai *birds*. About 1770. (11⅜×7⅞ in.)

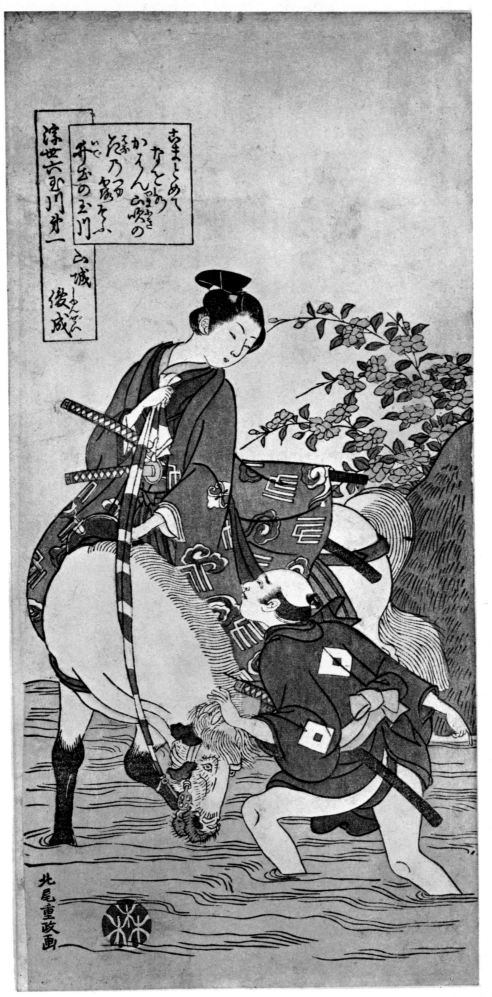

24. KITAO SHIGEMASA: *Youth on horseback being conducted across a ford.* ABOUT 1768. (12⅛ × 5½ in.)

25a. ISODA KORYŪSAI : *At the well*. About 1772. (25¾×4⅝ in.)

25b. TORII KIYONAGA : *Mother and servant with child beneath a willow tree*. About 1782. (24½×4⅝ in.)

26. KITAO SHIGEMASA: *Rehearsing a new song*. About 1777. (14⅞ × 10 in.)

27. Ippitsusai Bunchō: *The Telescope*. About 1770. (10×7½ in.)

28. KITAO SHIGEMASA : *Two geishas and a maid carrying a* koto (*musical instrument*) *box*. About 1777. Unsigned. (15 × 10¼ in.)

29. KATSUKAWA SHUNSHŌ: *Actor in character*. About 1771. (11⅔ × 5⅛ in.)

30. KITAO MASANOBU: *The mask*. Part of triptych. About 1783. (15 × 9⅞ in.)

石川豊雅画

31. ISHIKAWA TOYOMASA: *Boys feeding a stork*. About 1774. (9¾ × 7¼ in.)

32. TORII KIYONAGA: *The tea-house overlooking Shinagawa Bay*. Part of a diptych. About 1785. (15 × 10¼ in.)

33. TORII KIYONAGA : *A night of the Ninth Month*. Part of a diptych. About 1785. (15 × 10¼ in.)

34. TORII KIYONAGA : *Landing from the pleasure-barge.* Triptych. About 1786. (Each sheet 15 × 10 in.)

35. UTAGAWA TOYOHARU: *The Battle of Yashima, Dan-no-Ura. About 1775–1780. (9½ × 14¾ in.)*

36. TORII KIYONAGA: *Actors celebrating a festival.* 1788. (12⅛ × 5¼ in.)

37. Ippitsusai Bunchō: *The actor Segawa Kikunojō II in a female role.* About 1769. ($10\frac{3}{4} \times 4\frac{7}{8}$ in.)

38. TORII KIYONAGA : *The mediaeval poetess, Ono no Komachi*. About 1785. (15⅛×9⅞ in.)

39. KATSUKAWA SHUNSHŌ: *Scene from a play: Agemaki and her lover Sukeroku.* About 1780. ($15\frac{1}{4} \times 10\frac{3}{8}$ in.)

40. Katsukawa Shunkō: *Three actors in a scene from a mime*. About 1784. (15¼ × 10 in.)

鷺屋うち
菅原
むめの
えけの

栄し画

41. Chōbunsai Yeishi: *The courtesan Suguwara of Tsuru-ya and her attendants.* About 1789. (15¼ × 10¼ in.)

42. TORII KIYONAGA: *Cherry blossom at Asukayama near Yedo.* Part of a triptych. About 1788. (14¾×9½ in.)

東洲齋寫樂画

43. TOSHŪSAI SHARAKU : *Actors Kumajū Hangorō and Ichikawa Yawazō in character*. 1794. (14¼×9⅜ in.)

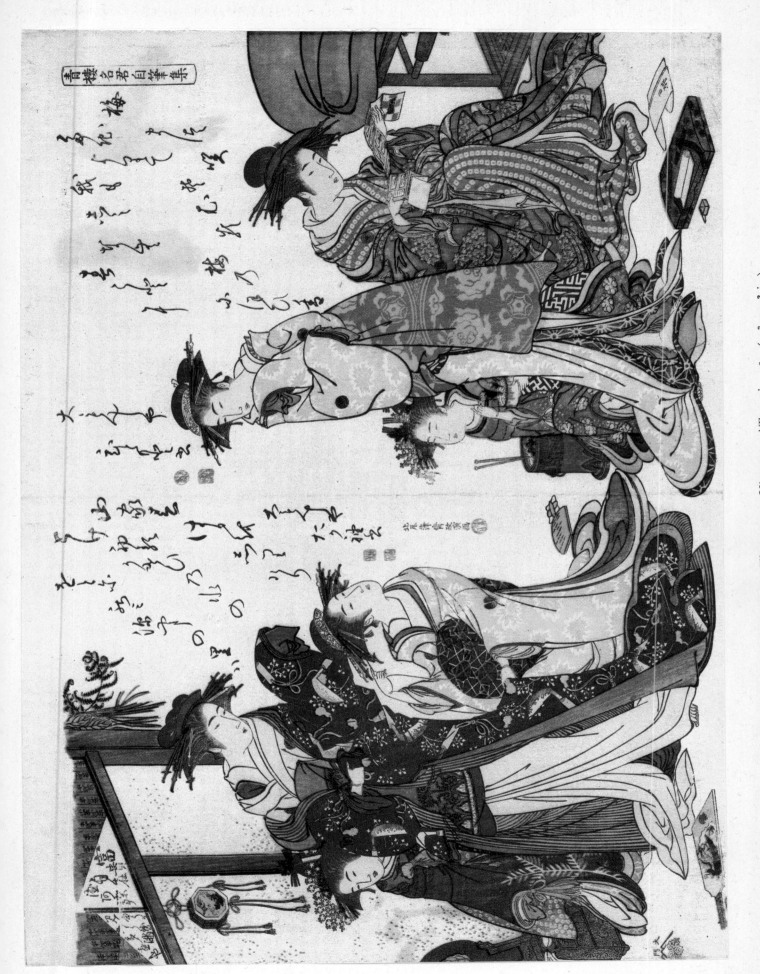

45. Kitao Masanobu: *The courtesans Hitomoto and Tagosode.* 1783. (14¾ × 19¾ in.)

46. KATSUKAWA SHUNZAN: *The hero Hachimantarō in battle.* About 1790. (14½ × 10¼ in.)

47. YEIRI : *Portrait of Santō Kyōden.* About 1795. (15 × 10 in.)

48. TOSHŪSAI SHARAKU: *The actor Kosagawa Tsuneyō in female character.* 1794. (14¼×9¼ in.)

49. Toshūsai Sharaku: *The actors Nakamura Gwanzō and Nukajima Watayeimon in character.* 1794. (14⅝×9 in.)

50. TOSHŪSAI SHARAKU: *Segawa Tomisaburō in female character.* 1794. (14¼×9⅜ in.)

51. Katsukawa Shunchō : *One of the 'Present-day Beauties of Nanboku'.* About 1790. (10⅜ × 14⅞ in.)

52. YEISHŌSAI CHŌKI : *Sunrise at the New Year*. About 1794. (13¼×9⅝ in.)

53. YEISHŌSAI CHŌKI: *Firefly-catching*. About 1794. (15×9⅞ in.)

54. CHŌBUNSAI YEISHI : *Scene from the 'Genji Romance'*. About 1792. Triptych. (Each sheet 14⅝ × 10 in.)

55. CHŌBUNSAI YEISHI: *The courtesan Nakagawa and her two attendants.* About 1796. (15¼ × 10 in.)

小野川
高嶋おひさ

春潮画

56. KATSUKAWA SHUNCHŌ: *The wrestler Onogawa and O-Hisa, a tea-house attendant.* About 1792. (15¼ × 10 in.)

57. KITAGAWA UTAMARO : *An outing on the banks of the Sumida River*. About 1788. (15 × 10 in.)

58. KUBŌ SHUNMAN: *The Tōi, one of the six Jewel-rivers*. About 1790. Part of a six-sheet composition. (14½ × 9¾ in.)

59. Kitagawa Utamaro: *Girl examining a piece of gauze*. About 1790. (15 × 10 in.)

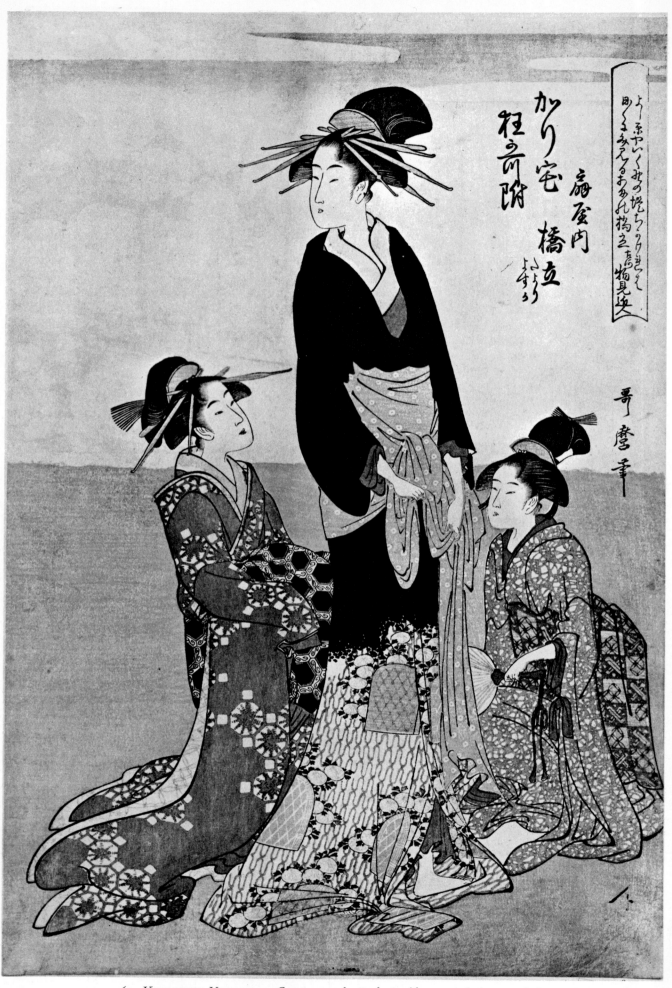

60. KITAGAWA UTAMARO: *Courtesan and attendants.* About 1796. (15 × 10 in.)

子
刻

青
楼
十
二
時
續

歌
麿
筆

61. KITAGAWA UTAMARO: *The Hour of the Rat—Midnight.* About 1795. (15 × 10 in.)

62. Utagawa Kunimasa : *The love-letter: a scene from a play*. About 1797. (15 × 10 in.)

63. YEISHŌ: *The courtesan Kasaganō of Sasaya.* About 1795. (14¾ × 10¼ in.)

郭中美人競

越前屋
唐土

泝里画

64. YEIRI: *The courtesan Morokoshi of Echizenya.* About 1795. (15 × 10¼ in.)

瀧ノ音　　　谷風

春英画

65. KATSUKAWA SHUNYEI: *The wrestler Tanikaze and his pupil Taki no Oto*. About 1796. (14⅞ × 9⅞ in.)

66. UTAGAWA TOYOKUNI: *The Fourth Month.* About 1795. (15 × 10 in.)

67. UTAGAWA TOYOHIRO: *Hawk*. About 1798. (15 × 9¾ in.)

68. UTAGAWA TOYOKUNI: *Otani Tomoyemon in character*. 1801. (15 × 10 in.)

69. HOKUSAI: *The waterfall of Yoshino.* About 1830. (15 × 10 in.)

70. HOKUSAI: *Fuji in clear weather.* About 1823–9. (10⅜ × 15⅛ in.)

名所江戸百景

堀切の花菖蒲

広重画

下谷
新黒魚栄

71. HIROSHIGE : *The Iris Garden at Horikiri.* 1857. (8⅝ × 13¼ in.)

72. HOKUSAI: *Cuckoo and azalea.* About 1828. (10 × 7¼ in.)

73. Hokusai : *Dragon-fly and Kikyō flowers.* About 1830. (10⅜ × 15 in.)

74. HOKUSAI: *Lilies*. About 1830. (10⅝ × 15 in.)

75. HOKUSAI: *Tamagawa, Musashi*. About 1823–9. (9¾ × 14⅞ in.)

76. Hiroshige: *Oi*. About 1840. ($8\frac{5}{8} \times 13\frac{5}{8}$ in.)

77. Hiroshige: *Miyanokoshi.* About 1840. (8⅝ × 13 in.)

78. KUNISADA: *The Cat Monster of Okabe*. About 1852. (14½ × 10 in.)

79. KUNIYOSHI : *Cats masquerading as actors*. About 1840. Fan-mount (*uchiwa*).

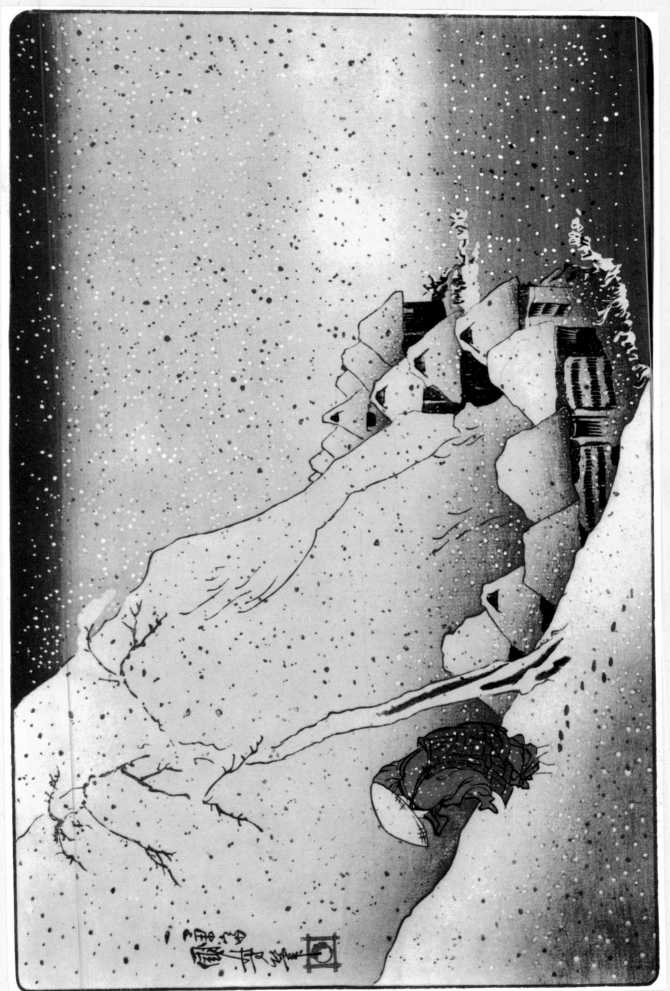

80. KUNIYOSHI: *Nichiren in the snow.* About 1835. (8¾×13½ in.)

NOTES ON THE ARTISTS AND THE ILLUSTRATIONS

Note: Biographical data are scarce even in respect of the major artists, and in respect of others are sometimes entirely lacking. It has been considered sufficient merely to name minor artists in the chronological sequence, attaching them to the master with whom they have closest affinities. In an appendix like this, it would be out of place to give the family names, and the often numerous 'art-names', of each artist. Instead, except in a few instances, only the name by which the artist is commonly known, and which is most often signed on the prints, has been given.

HISHIKAWA MORONOBU (1625–1694). After following for a time the calling of his father, an embroiderer, he received some training as a painter in both the Tosa and Kano schools. However, although not a direct pupil of Matahei, as early as 1658 his illustrations to a book show the influence of the founder of the Ukiyo-ye School, who died in 1650. During the remaining years of his life, Moronobu illustrated over one-hundred books and designed numerous separate broadsheets, setting a style of drawing for the woodcut which affected the work of all the subsequent Ukiyo-ye print-designers. Of Moronobu's own pupils, Morofusa and Moroshige were the most successful in reproducing the master's style.

Plate 2: *Returning from a flower-picnic.* One of a series 'The Fashion of Flower-viewing at Uyeno'. Unsigned. Ink-print, hand-coloured. $10\frac{1}{2} \times 16\frac{1}{8}$ in. *c.* 1675. (British Museum.)

Figure 1: A page from the picture-book *Musashi Yehon.* 8×6 in. *c.* 1680. (British Museum.)

TORII KIYONOBU I (1664–1729) came of an Osaka theatrical family, and assisted his father in painting signboards for the theatre in Yedo, to which town the family moved in 1687. Soon after, Kiyonobu began illustrating books, and about 1695 designed the first actor-prints, which were immediately successful with the Yedo public. His treatment in these early prints is broad and suggests the signboard artist, though his style owed much to Moronobu. He is the founder of the Torii family of artists, noted principally for actor-prints. His late work cannot be separated with certainty from that of the second Kiyonobu, but the earlier has a swirl and frenzy of design that is entirely individual. His broadsheets are all ink-prints (*sumi-ye*), with or without the addition of hand-colouring.

Plate 4: *Two actors in the play called 'Saya-ate'.* Ink-print. $10\frac{1}{4} \times 5\frac{3}{4}$ in. *c.* 1700. (British Museum.)

KIYOTADA (worked first half of 18th century) was a pupil of Kiyonobu I.

KATSUKAWA TERUSHIGE, of whom little is known, was apparently a pupil of Kiyonobu I, and is known by a few rare prints of unusual merit.

SUGIMURA JIHEI (active late 17th and early 18th century). Very little is known of this contemporary of Moronobu. His work comprises a number of prints and albums, mostly of erotic contents, that appeared between 1685–1698. His style is close enough to Moronobu's for his prints to have been ascribed to that master, some having been identified only when one of his own names, Masataka, was found worked into the design. He makes most effective use of the disposition of the blacks in conjunction with a rich linear decoration.

Plate 3: *Lovers discovered behind a screen.* A page from an album. $14\frac{1}{2} \times 10\frac{1}{2}$ in. *c.* 1690. (F. Tikotin Collection.)

KWAIGETSUDŌ (active early 18th century). The rare and beautiful prints signed with this name are taken to be the work either of four artists, pupils of one Kwaigetsudō Ando; or, more plausibly, of one man who, like Hokusai, varied his 'personal' name in a capricious way. The identity of style in both drawing and hand-writing seems to rule out the theory of a number of artists. Kwaigetsudō was living in Yedo between 1704 and 1716, and his extant works appear to belong to that period. His prints, almost invariably of a single courtesan in heavy robes patterned with the then fashionable large motifs, are among the most impressive of the whole range of Japanese art.

Plate 1: *Courtesan playing with a cat.* Ink-print (*sumi-ye*). *c.* 1710. (Morse Collection, Wadsworth Atheneum, Hartford, U.S.A.)

NISHIKAWA SUKENOBU (1674–1754). Separately issued prints by this master are rare: his immense output was almost entirely confined to illustrated books published in Kyōto and Osaka, from about 1710 until his death. Generally, these have poetic titles that give little indication of the contents, but his books are invariably concerned with the lives of young women, virtuous or otherwise, their daily occupations, the fashions and customs of the day. His drawing, though influenced by Moronobu, Kwaigetsudō and Kiyonobu, is milder than theirs, the primitive roughness smoothed over. His style is a link between Moronobu and Harunobu.

Figure 2: Double page from a picture-book of the occupations of women, *Yehon Tokiwa Gusa*. 8½ × 13½ in. 1731. (British Museum.)

TORII KIYOMASU I (1696?–1716?).
TORII KIYONOBU II (b. 1702–1752?).
TORII KIYOMASU II (1706–1763).
Modern scholarship contrives to make two Kiyomasu, as it has already made two Kiyonobu. The first Kiyomasu was short-lived. The second Kiyonobu, who took over the name when the first retired in 1729, was a younger son of the master; Kiyomasu II took over that name upon the death of the first Kiyomasu. All this is very confusing, but of little import. The style of all three is typical of the Torii School, and is seen to pass through several phases: the truly primitive ink-prints, often hand-coloured; lacquer prints; and, in the last stages, two-colour prints. Their work was devoted almost entirely to the stage.

Plate 5: *Arashi Wakano as the poetess Ono no Komachi, dancing*. Hand-coloured lacquer-print. 10¾ × 6⅛ in. Publisher: Igayo. *c.* 1715. (British Museum.)

Plate 13: *The actor Onoye Kikujorō as a courtier dancing*. Print in green and rose. 11⅞ × 5½ in. Publisher: Yemiya Kichiyemon. *c.* 1745. (British Museum.)

KIYOSHIGE (active 1716–1760) produced some powerful actor prints in black outline, alone or with boldly decorative hand-colouring.

OKUMURA MASANOBU (1686–1764). One of the central figures of the colour-print movement. Moronobu, Kwaigetsudō and Sukenobu all had their share in the formation of his style, though he is not known to have been the pupil of any one of them. Though at times designing stage-prints, he found his material, like Sukenobu, principally in the social life around him. As a bookseller in Yedo, he knew better than most what the new public desired and was always in the van with innovations, with eye-catching devices. He is accredited with the introduction of lacquer-prints and *Uki-ye* ('perspective pictures') and was one of the first to design for the two-colour prints. He covers almost the whole of the Primitive period, beginning with the large-scale ink-prints owing much to Kwaigetsudō's model, and ending with *beni-ye* that in their graceful drawing and poetic sentiment, point the way to Harunobu.

Plate 6: *Courtesan*. Woodcut in white line on black in imitation of the Chinese stone-prints used for making outline copies of famous pictures (*Ishi-zuri-ye*). 16¾ × 11½ in. *c.* 1705. (F. Tikotin Collection.)

Plate 7: *An actor as a girl dancing*. 12 × 8½ in. *c.* 1715. (British Museum.)

Plate 12: *The Love-Letter*. Hand-coloured print. 24 × 9¾ in. *c.* 1748. (British Museum.)

OKUMURA TOSHINOBU (active 1725–1750), a pupil of Masanobu, designed a few enchanting lacquer-prints.

Plate 10: *Actors as a flower-seller and a street musician*. Hand-coloured lacquer-print. 13 × 6¼ in. *c.* 1740. (British Museum.)

MANGETSUDŌ was another gifted pupil of Okumura Masanobu.

TORII KIYOHIRO (active 1737–1768), a pupil of Kiyomasu II, was, like most members of the Torii family, mainly a designer of theatrical prints. Hand-coloured prints and lacquer-prints by him are known, but he was at his best in the *beni-ye* print. He has a piquancy of line and motive that singles him out from his fellow Torii artists, who were inclined to be if anything a little conservative.

Plate 9: *Children spinning tops*. Print in green and rose. 17 × 11⅞ in. Publisher: Maruya. *c.* 1745. (British Museum.)

TORII KIYOMITSU (1735–1785). A son and pupil of Kiyomasu II, he was one of the most prominent artists of the period from 1730 to 1764, and one of the first to experiment with three- and four-block printing, and the colours obtainable from over-printings. His prints in the narrow upright format (*hoso-ye*) may be slightly monotonous in the repetition of certain mannerisms, but his pillar-prints are superb, and include a number in which the nude or half-draped figure is depicted with a grace in drawing the human form that is as delightful as it is surprising.

Plate 15: *Actors as lovers in a play*. Print in three colours. 17¼ × 12⅛ in. Publisher: Yeijudō. 1765. (British Museum.)

TORII KIYOTSUNE (active *c.* 1757–*c.* 1771). A pupil of Kiyomitsu, he worked much in his master's manner. He is chiefly distinguishable by the expression of fastidious disdain worn by most of the faces he drew.

NISHIMURA SHIGENAGA (1697–1756). A book- and print-seller himself, Shigenaga was another of those artists who kept pace with the changing demands of his patrons. Beginning in the early manner of Masanobu with hand-coloured prints that never warranted his disparagement as 'a faded and weakened Masanobu', his two-coloured prints have a touch of fancifulness, 'an odd way of bringing grace out of apparent awkwardness', that explains in part their attraction for us. Among his pupils were Toyonobu, Harunobu, Shigemasa and possibly Koryūsai—sufficient claim to fame if he had no other. He is the bridge between the Primitive period of *sumi-ye* and two-coloured prints, and the full-colour period inaugurated by Harunobu in 1764.

Plate 8: *The actor Sanjo Kantarō as a Tea-seller*. Hand-coloured lacquer-print. 13 × 6¼ in. Igaya. *c.* 1725. (British Museum.)

YAMAMOTO YOSHINOBU (worked 1750–1775). One of a number of obscure artists of this family. Probably a pupil of Shigenaga.

ISHIKAWA TOYONOBU (1711–1785). Beginning as a pupil of Shigenaga under the name of Nishimura Shigenobu, and issuing his first hand-coloured prints under that name, soon after 1737 he changed his name to Toyonobu. Prints so signed are among the finest of the 'primitives', though as applied to him the term has already lost much of its significance. True, among his earlier prints, the splendid *kakemono-ye* show a debt more to Masanobu than to Shigenaga, but with the coming of the *beni-ye*, the poetry in the air of Yedo was instilled into his prints, and some Japanese critics, Noguchi, for instance, who calls him the 'lyric poet of Ukiyo-ye', look upon his work as the high-water mark of the whole colour-print movement. He continued working into the era of full polychrome printing, but by that time was over-shadowed by Harunobu.

Plate 11A: *A Korean Envoy*. Hand-coloured ink print. 26¼ × 6 in. *c.* 1740. (British Museum.)

Plate 11B: *Girl closing an umbrella*. Print in three colours. 26½ × 4¼ in. Publisher: Moriya. *c.* 1760. (British Museum.)

Plate 14: *Boy dancing with a hobby-horse*. Print in green and rose. 17 × 12 in. Publisher: Maruya. *c.* 1755. (British Museum.)

ISHIKAWA TOYOMASA (active 1767–1773) was a pupil of Toyonobu.

Plate 31: *Boys feeding a stork*. 9¾ × 7¼ in. *c.* 1773. (British Museum.)

SUZUKI HARUNOBU (d. 1770). Little is known of this artist's early years. A contemporary has left it on record that Harunobu was over forty when he died. He was a pupil of Shigenaga, and designed a few two-colour prints before introducing, or at least developing, the full colour-print. With the enhanced possibilities of the new technique came an astonishing advance in his powers. He exemplifies one side of the Japanese colour-print's charm—the depiction of a world of diminutive graceful creatures, an idyllic world where work is never taken seriously, and play is the real business of life. The prints are sure in drawing, and coloured with tints so exquisite that Harunobu has been credited with a greater share in the development of the true *nishiki-ye*, the brocade-print, than anyone else. His output was immense considering the short space of time that encompassed it: but it is likely that many prints signed with his name can be ascribed either to talented pupils, or to forgers. His colour-print illustrated books, of which one dated 1770, 'Beauties of the Green-Houses' is outstanding, were among the first of their kind.

Pupils or followers of Harunobu were Harushige, Harutsugu, Komai Yoshinobu, Masunobu, Minkō, Kuninobu, Fujinobu.

Plate 16: *The Summer Shower*. One of the earliest polychrome prints, a Calendar print for 1765. It bears four signatures. Gwakō (designer) Suzuki Harunobu; Chōkō (engraver) Endo Goryoku; Senkō (printer) Yumoto Sachiye; and Hakusai, who probably supplied the idea for the picture. 1765. (Morse Collection, Wadsworth Atheneum, Hartford, U.S.A.)

Plate 17A: *A Courtesan looking at the moon's reflection*. One of a set of 'Popular Six Jewel-rivers'. On the title panel is a poem by Toshiyori, whose portrait is given in the square inset. 27 × 4½ in. *c.* 1768. (British Museum.)

Plate 17B: *Lovers sharing an umbrella*. 26½ × 4⅞ in. *c.* 1770. (Morse Collection, Wadsworth Atheneum, Hartford, U.S.A.)

Plate 18: *The Sacred White Horse*. 10⅞ × 8¼ in. *c.* 1767. (British Museum.)

Plate 19: *Girls fording a stream*. From a set of 'Six Jewel Rivers', this one representing Hagi no Tamagawa Yamashiro. Unsigned. 9¾ × 7⅛ in. *c.* 1766. (British Museum.)

ISODA KORYŪSAI (active *c.* 1764 to 1780) came of *samurai* stock, but forsook the service of a nobleman to study Ukiyo-ye painting. His first master was Shigenaga, and it is said that he afterwards worked under Harunobu, whose influence, certainly, is paramount in his early prints of small size, prints which, apart from showing a preference for certain individual colour schemes, can only be separated from Harunobu's with difficulty. But Koryūsai was far more than an imitator: his *kwachō* are of supremely fine design, his *hashirakake* generally held to show the inventive composition of the Japanese artist at its best, and his great series of fashion-plates, 'New Patterns for Young Leaves' (a euphemism like Proust's 'les filles en fleur') designed with large-scale figures that show a reaction from the diminutive creatures of Harunobu's world, inaugurated the use of the large upright sheet which thereafter was in almost universal use by the designers of *bijin-ye* (pictures of beauties). After 1780, he devoted himself almost entirely to painting.

Plate 20: *Fashion Plate* from the series 'New Patterns for Young Leaves': *The courtesan Morokoshi of Echizenya*. 15¼ × 10 in. Yeijudō. *c.* 1775. (British Museum.)

Plate 21: *Man and girl on the verandah of a house*. 10 × 7¼ in. *c.* 1772. (Author's Collection.)

Plate 22: *Feeding Carp*. Unsigned. 9¾ × 7½ in. *c.* 1771. (British Museum.)

Plate 23: *Rai birds*. $11\frac{3}{8} \times 7\frac{7}{8}$ in. *c.* 1770. (British Museum.)

Plate 25A: *At the well*. $25\frac{3}{4} \times 4\frac{5}{8}$ in. *c.* 1772. (British Museum.)

Figure 3: *The toy sailing boat*. Hashirakake, $28\frac{1}{2} \times 4\frac{3}{4}$ in. *c.* 1772. (British Museum.)

KITAO SHIGEMASA (1739–1819). After Harunobu's death, and before Kiyonaga came to the fore, Shigemasa was perhaps the most commanding figure in Ukiyo-ye. Prints of such series as the 'Beauties of the East', often unsigned, show, like Koryūsai's, a reaction from the *petite* of Harunobu, the figures having an amplitude and a naturalism that make these designs among the most memorable of the period. Before this, probably a fellow pupil of Harunobu's in Shigenaga's studio, he drew in the Harunobu manner, and collaborated with Shunshō in one of the loveliest of all the colour-printed books, the 'Mirror of the Fair Women of the Green-Houses' of 1776; and after Kiyonaga's ascendancy, devoted himself largely to book-illustration, his separate sheets being uncommon. His long life carried him well into the 19th century, and he was still producing designs of a high quality almost to the end.

Plate 24: *Youth on horseback being conducted across a ford*. From a set 'A Ukiyo version of the Six Jewel Rivers'. $12\frac{1}{8} \times 5\frac{1}{2}$ in. Publisher: Moriji. *c.* 1768 (British Museum.)

Plate 26: *Rehearsing a new song*. A geisha holding an open song-book, whilst her companion tunes a *samisen*. Unsigned. Also known bearing the signature of Kitao Masanobu, but this is probably a later interpolation. $14\frac{7}{8} \times 10$ in. *c.* 1777. (British Museum.)

Plate 28: *Two Geishas and a maid carrying a* koto (musical instrument) *box*. Unsigned. $15 \times 10\frac{1}{4}$ in. *c.* 1777. (British Museum.)

Figure 4: A double page from the picture-book 'A Mirror of Rival Beauties'. $8\frac{1}{2} \times 11\frac{1}{2}$ in. 1776. (Author's Collection.)

KITAO MASANOBU (1761–1816). A pupil of Shigemasa, with uncommon precocity, he matched his master's finest designs whilst still in his early twenties, designed seven diptychs for an album 'The Autographs of Yoshiwara Beauties' (1783) that are among the most splendid creations of the Ukiyo-ye school, and then, when the leadership of the school seemed within his powers, forsook print-designing for writing, and under the name of Santō Kyōden, produced novels that are among the humorous classics of the Japanese literature. A true *Yedokkō*, a Yedo Cockney, he typifies the new class of commoner, with a gusto for the 'fast-life', for novelty, and for the beauty of the 'passing world'.

Plate 30: *The mask*: part of a triptych. $15 \times 9\frac{7}{8}$ in. *c.* 1783. (British Museum.)

Plate 44: *The call of the cuckoo*. $15\frac{1}{2} \times 22$ in. *c.* 1782. (Museum of Fine Arts, Boston, Mass.)

Plate 45: *The courtesans Hitomoto and Tagosode*. Double page print from the album 'The Autographs of Yoshiwara Beauties'. $14\frac{3}{4} \times 19\frac{3}{4}$ in. Publisher: Tsutajū. 1783. (British Museum.)

KITAO MASAYOSHI (1761–1824). Another pupil of Shigemasa. After some promising prints in the Ukiyo-ye style, he seceded to the Kano, and is chiefly remembered for book illustrations consisting of summary sketches of great verve, and birds and flowers printed without outlines.

KATSUKAWA SHUNSHŌ (1726–1792). Trained in a sub-school of Ukiyo-ye that confined itself to painting, Shunshō began with prints that owe something to the all-pervading influence of Harunobu, but after collaborating with Shigemasa in the book already mentioned and in a series of prints dealing with sericulture, he found his true vein in the theatrical print at a time when the Torii family was in a partial eclipse. His countless actor prints of the *hoso-ye* format are composed with a rare restraint of colour and design, and succeed in bringing the Japanese stage to life before our eyes. But they are only one side of his work: he is equally great in all the other spheres of the colour-print designer, though one of the most conservative and least innovating.

Plate 29: *Actor in character*. $11\frac{2}{8} \times 5\frac{1}{3}$ in. *c.* 1771. (F. Tikotin Collection.)

Plate 39: *Scene from a play*. *Agemaki and her lover Sukeroku*. $15\frac{1}{4} \times 10\frac{3}{4}$ in. *c.* 1780. (British Museum.)

Figure 6: *The actor Danjuro V in character*. 10×5 in. *c.* 1780. (F. Tikotin Collection.)

IPPITSUSAI BUNCHŌ (active *c.* 1760–1779). Another artist of the *samurai* class, Bunchō seceded from the Kano school and devoted himself, like Shunshō, to the stage. His actor-prints stand apart from all others in their extreme elegance of drawing and a disquieting emotional quality that affects us like a poignant discord in music. In 1770 he collaborated with Shunshō in the 'Book of Stage Fans', a collection of portraits of actors in fan-shaped frames, one of the finest of the earlier *yehon*. Like so many other Ukiyo-ye artists—Toyonobu, Shunman, Kitao Masanobu are a few—he was a poet of some standing.

Plate 27: *The telescope*: one of a series of eight views of the Sumida River. $10 \times 7\frac{1}{2}$ in. *c.* 1770. (British Museum.)

Plate 37: *The actor Segawa Kikunojō II in a female rôle*. $10\frac{3}{4} \times 4\frac{7}{8}$ in. *c.* 1769. (British Museum.)

KATSUKAWA SHUNKŌ (d. 1827). A close follower of his master, Shunshō. His actor prints have the same admirable qualities, and but for the signature, would often be difficult to distinguish from his master's. Paralysis attacked him in middle age and prevented him from realizing his early promise.

Plate 40: *Three actors in a scene from a mime produced in the Kiri-za theatre in 1784.* 15¼ × 10 in. *c.* 1784. (British Museum.)

KATSUKAWA SHUNYEI (1768–1819). Another pupil of Shunshō with more marked individuality than Shunkō. His actor prints show affinities with Shunshō's, but even in these his originality comes out in a predilection for strong, macabre designs and sombre colour schemes. He is credited with being the first to draw large portrait heads of the kind Sharaku and Utamaro made their own, and he also excelled in prints of wrestlers, who were fêted by the Yedo crowds as the professional boxer is among us. Altogether, Shunyei is one of the most talented artists of the late 18th century.
Shunyei's pupils include Shuntei and Kashōsai Shunsen.

Plate 65: *The wrestler Tanikaze and his pupil Taki no Oto.* 14⅞ × 9⅞ in. Publisher: Tsuruya. *c.* 1796. (British Museum.)
Other pupils of Shunshō include Shundō, Shunjō, Shunyoku, Shunrin, Shunkwaku, Katsukawa Shunsen and Shunkyō.

UTAGAWA TOYOHARU (1733–1814). Most probably an early pupil of Sekiyen, Toyoharu's first prints were designed whilst Harunobu's influence still remained, and his pillar prints of this period and a little later are very fine. Later, he developed the *uki-ye* type of perspective picture which combines European and Japanese elements in an intriguing manner. He is the founder of the Utagawa line of artists; Toyokuni and Toyohiro were his major pupils. Toyohisa and Toyomaru were other pupils.

Plate 35: *The Battle of Yashima, Dan-no-Ura.* An event in the civil war between the Minamoto and Taira clans. *Uki-ye* print. 9½ × 14¾ in. Publisher: Yeijudō. *c.* 1775–1780. (British Museum.)

TORII KIYONAGA (1752–1815). Coming to Yedo when a young man as a follower of the trade of tobacconist and bookseller, Kiyonaga was adopted into the Torii family, and became the pupil of Kiyomitsu. His early work up to about 1780 follows the Torii actor-print style and there are lingering traces of Harunobu and Koryūsai; but with the eighties, Kiyonaga seemed suddenly to find his feet, and he produced series after series of prints that are among the classics of Ukiyo-ye art. The most famous are called 'Brocade of the East (Yedo) in Fashion' and twelve diptychs entitled 'Twelve months of the South'. These, and similar prints, of the Yedo round of pleasure, with an increasing emphasis on the open air, the atmosphere and scenery of the town and its purlieus, are characterized at their culminating point by immensely tall figures of regal proportions,

welded into monumental designs, often processional, like a frieze; drawn with a mastery that few Ukiyo-ye artists rival. As the decade waned, the figures returned to more normal height, and there is something generally less imposing about the later prints, as if the fires of genius had been damped down. His influence on his contemporaries was enormous, comparable to Harunobu's over *his* generation of artists, every designer of note falling under his spell to a greater or lesser degree. Soon after 1790, he seems to have given up print-designing to return to his shop-keeping.
Kiyonaga's pupils include Kiyohisa and Kiyomasa, but his closest followers are Shunchō, Shunzan and Shunman, mentioned below, and Banki, Banri, Ryū-unsai and Yenshi.

Plate 25B: *Mother and servant with child beneath a willow tree.* 24½ × 4⅝ in. *c.* 1782. (British Museum.)

Plate 32: *The tea-house overlooking Shinagawa Bay:* left-hand sheet of a diptych from the series 'Twelve months in the South'. 15 × 10¼ in. *c.* 1785. (British Museum.)

Plate 33: *A night of the Ninth Month:* right-hand sheet of a diptych from the series 'Twelve months in the South'. 15 × 10¼ in. *c.* 1785. (Museum of Fine Arts, Boston, U.S.A.)

Plate 34: *Landing from the pleasure barge.* Triptych. Each sheet 15 × 10 in. *c.* 1786. (British Museum.)

Plate 36: *Actors celebrating a festival at the Shrine of the Soga Brothers.* The Soga Brothers are venerated as exemplars of filial devotion for revenging the death of their father at the hands of one Suketsune. Part of a pentaptych. 12⅛ × 5¼ in. 1788. (British Museum.)

Plate 38: *The mediaeval poetess, Ono no Komachi.* 15⅛ × 9⅞ in. *c.* 1785. (British Museum.)

Plate 42: *Cherry blossom at Asukayama near Yedo.* Centre sheet of a triptych. 14¾ × 9½ in. *c.* 1788. (British Museum.)

Figure 5: *Autumn moon on the Sumida river.* Part of a five-sheet print. 14¾ × 10 in. *c.* 1787. (British Museum.)

KITAGAWA UTAMARO (1753–1806). When Kiyonaga retired, Utamaro was ready to assume the leadership of Ukiyo-ye. Of practically the same age as Kiyonaga, Utamaro was slower to develop and had a different training, partly in the Kano School, partly under Sekiyen, who was not a true Ukiyo-ye artist. Influenced first by Shigemasa and Kitao Masanobu, and then by Kiyonaga, Utamaro was never a copyist but showed individuality from the start. In 1788, his 'Insect Book', a wonderful set of prints of flowers and insects and birds, was published, and it was followed by other albums of great charm, containing prints which are pure landscape. His mature powers, however, were devoted to the women of the Yoshiwara, and his prolific output in the nineties contains prints that are among the masterpieces of the colour woodcut. With the turn of the century, his art, infected by the spirit of the age and the need to satisfy insatiable publishers, deteriorated, and many prints of this late period issued under his name are the work of pupils or forgers. He died in 1806 not long after an imprisonment for an infringement of the censorship laws had finally broken a constitution already impaired, so tradition declares, by dissipation.

Pupils and followers include: Utamaro II, who forged his signature; Shikimaro, Kikumaro (also called Tsukimaro) Hidemaro, Bunrō, Banki II, Hisanobu, Ryūkoku.

Plate 57: *An outing on the banks of the Sumida River.* 15 × 10 in. Publisher: Tsutajū. *c.* 1788. (Musée Guimet.)

Plate 59: *Girl examining a piece of gauze.* 15 × 10 in. Publisher: Tobei. *c.* 1790. (Musée Guimet.)

Plate 60: *Courtesan and attendants.* 15 × 10 in. Publisher: Tobei. *c.* 1796. (British Museum.)

Plate 61: *The Hour of the Rat—Midnight*: from the set 'The Twelve Hours of the Green-Houses'. 15 × 10 in. Publisher: Tsutajū. *c.* 1795. (British Museum.)

Figure 8: *Cicada and snail with fruit and plants.* A double page from the 'Insect Book'. Publisher: Tsutajū. 1788. 10 × 15 in. (British Museum.)

SEKIJŌ and SEKIHŌ were also pupils of Sekiyen, but worked much under the influence of Utamaro.

KATSUKAWA SHUNCHŌ. Apart from the fact that he was a pupil of Shunshō, nothing is known of his life, and his personality is almost completely overshadowed by that of Kiyonaga, whose style, after breaking with Shunshō, he followed with complete fidelity. In his colouring, and in his pillar-print designing, it is possible to detect an individual note, but it is never heard solo, it is always in duet with Kiyonaga's.

Plate 51: *One of the 'Present-day Beauties of Nanboku'.* 10⅜ × 14⅞ in. Publisher: Fushimiya. *c.* 1790. (British Museum.)

Plate 56: *The wrestler Onogawa and O-Hisa, a tea-house attendant.* 15¼ × 10 in. Publisher: Tsuruya. *c.* 1792. (British Museum.)

Figure 7: *Girl by the Sacred Pine.* Hashirakake. 27¼ × 4⅞ in. *c.* 1789. Publisher: Yeiyudo. (British Museum.)

SHUNZAN (active 1780–1800). Another apostate from Shunshō's academy to Kiyonaga's, Shunzan's history is obscure. Fine prints exist from the period of his tutelage under Shunshō and Shunyei, but his best work was done in direct emulation of Kiyonaga, whose style he cleverly assimilated.

Plate 46: *The hero Hachimantaro in battle.* 14½ × 10¼ in. Publisher: Mikawaya. *c.* 1790. (British Museum.)

KUBO SHUNMAN (1757–1820). After an initial training under obscure painters, he studied Ukiyo-ye under Shigemasa (he was never a pupil of Shunshō as his name might suggest), but soon succumbed to the influence of Kiyonaga. But unlike Shunchō, he retained his own identity, attaining a degree of refinement in everything he did which places his relatively small output in a category of its own. He was an experimenter in colour, using silvery greys and light touches of colour with exquisite results (his most famous work, the six-sheet print of the 'Six Jewel Rivers' is a perfect example); and excelled in *surimono*, and in the illustration of books of poetry. He himself was a notable poet, and his poetry seems to have overflowed into his designing.

Plate 58: *The Tōi, one of the Six Jewel-rivers.* Part of a six-sheet composition. 14½ × 9¾ in. Publisher: Fushizen. *c.* 1790. (British Museum.)

CHŌBUNSAI YEISHI (1756–1829). One of the few Ukiyo-ye artists who could claim gentle descent, he forsook the Kano School and took Kiyonaga as his model. He found the tall forms affected by Kiyonaga at one period particularly engaging, and, like Utamaro, wilfully exaggerated the height and slimness of his courtesan models and produced designs of a rare elegance. His triptychs of 'Genji in Modern Dress' are perhaps his greatest triumphs. After 1800 he gave himself up to painting, in which sphere he proved himself one of the greatest of the school.

Plate 41: *The courtesan Suguwara of Tsuru-ya and her attendants.* 15¼ × 10¼ in. *c.* 1789. (British Museum.)

Plate 54: *Scene from the 'Genji Romance'.* Triptych, each sheet 14⅝ × 10 in. Publisher: Yeijudō. *c.* 1792. (British Museum.)

Plate 55: *The courtesan Nakagawa and her two attendants.* 15¼ × 10 in. Publisher: Yeijudō. *c.* 1796. (British Museum.)

CHŌKŌSAI YEISHŌ (active 1780–1800). As is the case with so many Ukiyo-ye artists, practically no biographical details exist concerning Yeishō. He closely followed his master Yeishi, eschewing the stage, concentrating on the courtesans' world, and designing some 'large heads' which seem to owe a debt to Utamaro.

Plate 63: *The courtesan Kasuganō of Sasaya.* One of a set 'Rival Beauties of the Yoshiwara'. 14¾ × 10¼ in. Publisher: Tobei. *c.* 1795. (British Museum.)

ICHIRAKUTEI YEISUI worked at the same time and in the same manner as Yeishō.

YEIRI (worked 1789–1800). Although a follower of Yeishi, his few and rare prints have a strong individuality.

Plate 47: *Portrait of Santō Kyōden* (the name the artist

Kitao Masanobu used as a writer). 15 × 10 in. *c.* 1795. (Museum of Fine Arts, Boston, Mass., U.S.A.)

Plate 64: *The courtesan Morokoshi of Echizenya.* One of the set 'Rival Beauties of the Yoshiwara'. 15 × 10¼ in. Publisher: Tobei. *c.* 1795. (British Museum.)

REKISENTEI YEIRI (active 1780–1800). Although not a direct pupil of Yeishi (his name is written with a different character for *yei*), he had obviously close affinities to that artist and his followers.
Other pupils and followers of Yeishi were Gokyō, Yeishin, Yeiju, and Yeiryū.

TAMAGAWA SHŪCHŌ (worked 1790–1805) designed prints in Yeishi's manner.

TŌSHŪSAI SHARAKU (d. 1801). Originally an actor in the Nō drama, the appearance of this dynamic artist in the Ukiyo-ye ranks is one of the mysteries of Japanese art. Without, so far as has been traced, previous training, he designed in 1794 a series of over one-hundred actor-prints under the imprint of Tsūtaya Jūsaburō, that are most powerfully original, whatever they may owe to the example of Shunshō and Shunyei. The large heads, in particular, at least as far as the type is concerned, were prompted by Shunyei, but the intensity of the drawing, the bizarre colour against the dark mica backgrounds, are without parallel in the annals of Ukiyo-ye. Presumably, the realism of these prints was not to the public's taste, for after his meteoric appearance, Sharaku returns to the obscurity from whence he had sprung.

Plate 43: *Actors Kumajū Hangorō and Ichikawa Yawazō in character.* 14¼ × 9⅜ in. Publisher: Tsutajū. 1794. (British Museum.)

Plate 48: *The actor Kosagawa Tsuneyō in female character.* 14¼ × 9¼ in. Publisher: Tsutajū. 1794. (British Museum.)

Plate 49: *The actors Nakamura Gwanzo and Nukajima Watayeimon in character.* 14⅝ × 9 in. Publisher: Tsutajū. 1794. (British Museum.)

Plate 50: *Segawa Tomisaburō in female character.* 14¼ × 9⅜ in. Publisher: Tsutajū. 1794. (British Museum.)

KABUKIDO YENKIO (worked 1789–1800). Designed portrait heads in imitation of Sharaku.

YEISHŌSAI CHŌKI (worked 1772–1795). A fellow-student with Utamaro under Sekiyen, at which time he bore the name Shikō, Chōki was influenced by Utamaro and Kiyonaga, and was one of the first to pay Sharaku the tribute of imitation. But the essential Chōki is confined to a handful of lovely prints, dated about 1794 and mostly with mica-grounds, which have what has been described as 'an emotional quality rare in Ukiyo-ye'. These prints, like Cotman's Greta drawings, are the truly original part of his work. About 1795, the name Shikō again appears on prints, but whether these are Chōki's, reverting to the use of a former name, or a pupil's work, is uncertain.

Plate 52: *Sunrise at the New Year.* 13¼ × 9⅝ in. Publisher: Tsutajū. *c.* 1794. (British Museum.)

Plate 53: *Firefly catching.* 15 × 9⅞ in. Publisher: Tsutajū. *c.* 1794. (British Museum.)

KATSUSHIKA HOKUSAI (1760–1849). Yedo-born, the son of a mirror-maker, he was apprenticed to a wood-engraver, but soon turned to designing. His first master was Shunshō, under whom his name was Shunrō. About 1777 his first illustrated book appeared, the forerunner of an enormous output in this field. His work covers almost every sphere of Ukiyo-ye activity, actor-prints in the Shunshō manner, *bijin-ye* with a Kiyonaga cast, and *surimono* of unsurpassed delicacy and invention; but his finest work is pre-eminently in the realm of landscape, especially in the great series that appeared after 1820—the 'Thirty-six Views of Fuji' the 'Waterfalls', the 'Bridges' and many others.
Hokusai's pupils are very numerous. The following are the most important: Shinsai, Hokkei, Hokujū, Yamagawa Shigenobu, Gakutei, Katsushika Taitō, Hokuba, Hokuga, Hoku-un, Hokuyei, Hokutei, Hokusui, Hoku-i.

Plate 69: *The waterfall of Yoshino.* From the series 'Going the Round of the Waterfalls of the Country'. 15 × 10 in. Publisher: Yeijudō *c.* 1830. (Author's Collection.)

Plate 70: *Fuji in clear weather.* From the series 'The Thirty-six Views of Fuji'. 10⅜ × 15⅛ in. Publisher: Yeijudō. *c.* 1823–1829. (British Museum.)

Plate 72: *Cuckoo and azalea.* From the series known as the 'Small Flowers'. 10 × 7¼ in. Publisher: Yeijudō. *c.* 1828. (British Museum.)

Plate 73: *Dragon-fly and kikyō flowers.* From the series known as the 'Large Flowers'. 10⅛ × 15 in. Publisher: Yeijudō. *c.* 1830. (British Museum.)

Plate 74: *Lilies.* From the same series as last. 10⅛ × 15 in. (British Museum.)

Plate 75: *Tamagawa, Musashi.* From the series 'The Thirty-six Views of Fuji'. 9¾ × 14⅛ in. *c.* 1823–1829. (British Museum.)

Figure 9: Page from the picture-book 'One hundred Views of Fuji'. 8 × 5½ in. 1835. (Author's Collection.)

UTAGAWA TOYOKUNI (1769–1825). A pupil of Toyoharu, he became the outstanding master of the Utagawa line. Influenced by Shunshō, Yeishi, Utamaro and Sharaku, he was an eclectic whose versions of those artists are always a little coarser than the originals. His most typical work is in the realm of the actor-print, of which he was the undisputed master after Shunshō and Sharaku had left the field. He came at an impropitious time, when standards of life and art were falling, and after the turn of the century, his style went rapidly downhill. His output was enormous—he illustrated over 350 books apart from designing a vast number of broadsheets—and his school comprised a large number of artists, much of whose work, belonging to the 19th century, exemplifies the debased standards of the period.

Frontispiece: *The actor Iwai Hanshiro in a feminine rôle.* From the series 'Actors as they appear on the stage'. In this series the influence of Sharaku is apparent. *c.* 1794. (Honolulu Academy of Arts, Hawaii, C. Montague Cooke Jr. Memorial Collection.)

Plate 66: *The Fourth Month.* One sheet of a triptych. From a series designed by Toyokuni and Toyohiro entitled 'The Twelve Months by Two Brushes'. 15 × 10 in. *c.* 1795. (F. Tikotin Collection.)

Plate 68: *Otani Tomoyemon in character.* 15 × 10 in. 1801. (British Museum.)

UTAGAWA TOYOHIRO (1763–1828). Eclipsed during his life by Toyokuni, his fellow pupil under Toyoharu, and remembered by later generations as the master of Hiroshige, Toyohiro's own contribution to the colour-print, even if a small one, is apt to be disregarded. His book illustrations, however, are of high quality, and in such prints as his 'Six Jewel Rivers', he shows a mastery in handling the landscape background which does much to explain his inspiration to Hiroshige.

Plate 67: *Hawk.* 15 × 9¾ in. *c.* 1798. (C. Rowe Collection.)

UTAGAWA KUNIMASA (active *c.* 1794–1810). One of Toyokuni's first pupils, Kunimasa assimilated Sharaku's style more thoroughly than his master, and his 'large heads' in particular are of great merit. He seems to have been active for a short period only, leaving print-designing to become a maker of masks.

Plate 62: *The love-letter.* A scene from a play. 15 × 10 in. *c.* 1797. (C. Rowe Collection.)

KUNISADA (1786–1864). Another pupil of Toyokuni, whose name he adopted in 1844 (being the third to bear the name, Toyoshige, an earlier pupil, having succeeded to it when Toyokuni died in 1825), Kunisada's career tells the tragedy of the downfall of Ukiyo-ye. With evident talent and tremendous verve, his early prints have qualities that link him with the great days of the school, but the great mass of his prints are hastily designed, over-coloured and badly printed.

Plate 78: *The Cat Monster of Okabe.* 14½ × 10 in. Publisher: Tsutaya Kichizō. *c.* 1852. (F. Tikotin Collection.)

KUNIYOSHI (1797–1861). This artist, again, shows an astonishing fecundity, and occasionally his prints, like those from the series illustrating scenes from the life of Nichiren, founder of a Buddhist sect, reach great heights. His illustrations to the heroic periods of Japanese history have great invention and gusto.

Plate 79: *Cats masquerading as actors.* Fan-mount (*uchiwa*). *c.* 1840. (B. W. Robinson Collection.)

Plate 80: *Nichiren in the snow.* From the series portraying the life of Nichiren, the founder of a Buddhist sect. 8¾ × 13½ in. Publisher: Iseiri. *c.* 1835. (F. Tikotin Collection.)

HIROSHIGE (1797–1858). Providentially, as we now see it, Hiroshige failed to gain admittance to Toyokuni's academy, and studied under Toyohiro instead. His early work, book-illustrations and figure designs, are not remarkable, but about 1826, his genius for landscape was made evident in a series of Yedo views, and confirmed beyond doubt in 1834 by the first of his series of prints of the 'Fifty-three Stations of the Tokaidō', the great highway between the new and old capitals, Yedo and Kyōto. From that time on, Hiroshige's industry in recording the beautiful Japanese scenery was astonishing, literally thousands of designs pouring from his brush. Among the most famous of the other series are the 'Eight Views of Lake Biwa'; the 'Sixty-nine Stations of the Kisakaidō'; 'Views of the Sixty-nine Provinces'; the 'One-hundred views of Yedo' and the 'Thirty-six Views of Fuji'. His *kwachō* and designs for fan-mounts are also noteworthy.

Plate 71: *The Iris Garden at Horikiri.* From the series 'The One-hundred Views of Yedo'. 8⅝ × 13¼ in. Publisher: Uoya Yeikichi. 1857. (British Museum.)

Plate 76. *Oi.* From the series 'The Sixty-nine Posting Stations of the Kisakaidō'. 8⅝ × 13⅝ in. Publisher: Kinjudō. *c.* 1840. (British Museum.)

Plate 77: *Miyanokoshi.* From the same series as last. 8⅝ × 13 in. Publisher: Kinjudō. *c.* 1840. (F. Tikotin Collection.)

Figure 12: Fan-mount (*uchiwa*): *Chrysanthemums, and a* kakemono *depicting a full moon.* (From a series 'Flower Arrangements of the Four Seasons'). 8½ × 11½ in. Publisher: Marukiken. *c.* 1835–40. (Victoria and Albert Museum.)

HIROKAGE was a pupil of Hiroshige.

HOKKEI (1780–1850), a pupil of Hokusai. His chief work was in book illustration and designs for *surimono*.

GAKUTEI (active first half of 19th century). A pupil of both Hokusai and Hokkei, Gakutei's output was confined almost entirely to *surimono*, though there is one fine landscape series from his hand.

Figure 10: *Carp leaping a water-fall.* Surimono. 8 × 7 in. *c.* 1840. (C. Rowe Collection.)

KEISAI YEISEN (1790–1848). Originally a pupil of the Kano School he went over to the Ukiyo-ye style. His pictures of beauties suffer from the falling standards of his time, but his landscapes often rival those of Hiroshige, with whom he collaborated in a notable series 'The Sixty-nine Stations of the Kisakaidō', the inland highway between Kyōto and Yedo.

Figure 11: *Inagawa Bridge, Nojiri*. From the series: 'The Sixty-nine Posting Stations of the Kisakaidō', 8½ × 13½ in. *c.* 1840. (Author's Collection.)

TEISAI SENCHO (worked 1830–1850) was a pupil of Yeisen and designed *bijin* in his manner.

KIKUGAWA YEIZAN (1787–1867). This artist's prints are confined largely to *bijin-ye* based on the later work of Utamaro, not a good model. Though successful in their day, they have few of the qualities that we look for in the colour-print of the masters.

HARUKAWA GOSHICHI (worked first half of 19th century) was mainly a *surimono* designer.

TORII KIYOMINE (1787–1869). One of the last of the great line of Torii artists, Kiyomine worthily upheld the traditions so rapidly being forsaken by his contemporaries. His prints of courtesans are of a surprisingly high quality considering their late date.
Pupils or followers of Toyokuni, Kunisada or Kuniyoshi who functioned in the last decades of the print are very numerous.
Those most likely to be encountered are: Kuninaga, Kunimitsu, Kunitsuna, Kunihisa, Kunikazu, Kunimori, Kunitomi, Kuniharu, Kuniyasu, Kunitane, Kuniteru,

Kuninao, Kuniaki, Kunichika, Kunihiko, Yoshitaki, Yoshiharu, Yoshikazu, Yoshimaru, Yoshitoshi, Sadakage, Sadafusa, Sadanobu, Sadahide, Sadahiro, Fusatane, Tominobu, Toyohide.

SUGAKUDŌ (worked mid-19th century) designed *kwachō* and is principally known by his set of 'Forty-eight Birds drawn from life' (1859).

KYŌSAI (1831–1889). An artist who carried something of the Ukiyo-ye manner into the latter half of the century. His drawing, mostly caricatural, is vigorous and often humorous.

THE OSAKA SCHOOL. In the first half of the 19th century colour-prints were produced in Osaka as well as in Yedo, and a local school of designers was established, influenced by both Hokusai and Kunisada, who are known to have spent some time in the town. The prints suffer from the same defects as the Yedo prints of the time, being badly designed and crudely coloured but they have at least the merit of being, as a rule, well printed. Some pupils of Kunisada are mentioned above; other Osaka artists are: Hokushu, Hokuyei, Hokusen, Shigeharu, Ashihiro, Ashiyuki, Ashimaro, Ashikiyo and Ashikuni. Matsukawa Hanzan also of Osaka, was a *surimono* designer of some ability.

SIGNATURES OF ARTISTS

Ashihiro	Ashiyuki	Bunchō	Gakutei	Harunobu	Hidemaro	Hisanobu	Hoku-I
Ashikiyo	Banki	Bunrō	Gokyō	Harushige	Hirokage	Hokkei	Hokujū
Ashikuni	Banki II	Chōki	Goshichi			Hokuba	Hokusai
Ashimaro	Banri	Fusatane	Hanzan	Harutsugu	Hiroshige	Hokuga	Hokushū

Hokutsui	Kiyomitsu		Kunimitsu	Kuniyasu	Kitao Masanobu	Sadahide	Shigeharu
Hokuyei	Kiyonaga	Kunichika	Kunimori	Kuniyoshi	Masayoshi	Sadahiro	Shigemasa
Keisai (Yeisen)	Kiyonobu	Kuniharu	Kuninaga		Masunobu	Sadakage	Shigenaga
Kikumaru	Kiyoshige	Kunihiko	Kuninao	Kwaigetsu (Kwaigetsudō)	Moronobu	Sadanobu	Shigenobu (afterwards Toyonobu)
Kiyohiro	Kiyotada	Kunihisa	Kunisada	Kyōsai	Morofusa	Sekihō	Shigenobu (Yanagawa)
Kiyomasa	Koryūsai	Kunikazu	Kuniteru	Mangetsudō	Ryūkoku	Sekijō	Shigenobu (Hiroshige II)
Kiyomasu	Kiyotsune	Kunimaru	Kunitomi		Ryū-unsai	Senchō	
Kiyomine	Kuniaki	Kunimasa	Kunitsuna	Okumura Masanobu	Sadafusa	Sharaku	Shikimaro

Shikō

Shinsai

Shūchō

Shunchō

Shundō

Shunjō

Shunkō

Shunkyō

Shunman

Shunrō
(later Hokusai)

Shunsen
(Katsukawa)

Shunsen
(Kashōsai)

Shunshō

Shuntei

Shunyei

Shunzan

Sōri (Hokusai)

Sugakudō

Sukenobu

Taitō
(Hokusai)

Terushige

Tominobu

Toshinobu

Toyoharu

Toyohide

Toyohiro

Toyohisa

Toyokuni
(also used by
Toyokuni II
(Toyoshige)
and
Toyokuni III
(Kunisada))

Toyomaru

Toyomasa

Toyonobu

Toyoshige

Tsukimaro

Utamaro

Yeiju

Yeiri

Yeiri
(Rekisentei)

Yeisen

Yeizan

Yeishi

Yeishō

Yeisui

Yenkyō

Yenshi

Yoshichika

Yoshiharu

Yoshikazu

Yoshikuni

Yoshimaru

Yoshinobu

Yoshitora

Yoshitoshi

Gwa   Fude   Dzu
(drew, painted, or designed)

ACKNOWLEDGEMENTS

Author and publisher are greatly indebted to Mr. Basil Gray, Keeper of the Department of Oriental Antiquities at the British Museum, who made available so many prints from the museum's superb collection and accorded permission to reproduce them as well as facilities for photography.

Sincere thanks are due also to the following private collectors and museum authorities who enabled us to reproduce prints in their possession: Mr. B. W. Robinson, London (plate 79); Mr. C. Rowe, Westbury (plates 62, 67, fig. 10); Mr. F. Tikotin, Wassenaar, Holland (plates 3, 6, 29, 66, 77, 78, 80, fig. 6); the Museum of Fine Arts, Boston, Mass. (plates 33, 44, 47, 49); Mrs. Morse and the Wadsworth Atheneum, Hartford, Conn. (plates 1, 16, 17b); the Honolulu Academy of Fine Arts, Honolulu, Hawaii (frontispiece); the Victoria and Albert Museum, London (fig. 12); and the Musée Guimet, Paris (plates 57, 59).